Quilting With A Difference

by Nikki Tinkler

Best wishes, Anne

— Nikki Tinkler

09/03

For Jim, Stephen and Jade

First published by
Traplet Publications Limited
Traplet House, Severn Drive, Upton upon Severn,
Worcestershire WR8 0JL

ISBN 1 900371 70 7
British Library Cataloguing in Publication Data
A catalogue record for this book is available from the British Library

Designed and edited by Teamwork, Christopher and Gail Lawther,
44 Rectory Walk, Sompting, Lancing, West Sussex BN15 0DU
Set in Giovanni and Gill Sans

Printed by Stephens & George
Goat Mill Road, Dowlais, Merthyr Tydfil CF48 3TD

Quilting With A Difference

Tradition with a twist
for lovers of hand-quilting

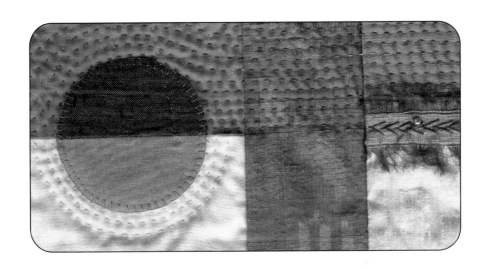

by Nikki Tinkler

T R A P L E T
PUBLICATIONS

Craftworld Series

❧ CONTENTS ❧

Introduction 6

the ins and outs of successful sewing　9

let's get stitching　27

projects　80

back to basics　123

A question:
when is quilting not quilting?

Photo: Jade Tinkler

I'VE pondered for quite a while now over this question – but I still have no definitive answer. Similarly, I've asked various needleworkers, both quilters and embroiderers, what they think about the so-called 'fine dividing line' between quilting and embroidery: is there a dividing line at all any more? And if so, where does quilting end and embroidery begin?

You can see from the examples in this book that the technique I call Quilting With A Difference is a combination of the two disciplines: I use embroidery stitches – in both traditional and contemporary styles – for quilting. My own theory is that, if the embroidery stitches are doing the actual job of quilting (ie passing through, and holding together, three layers) then the stitching can be classed as quilting, irrespective of its shape, size or appearance. At heart, I know that I'm happier making quilts rather than working embroidery – so perhaps that's the ultimate answer to my initial question.

This book is not meant to be a lesson in embroidery, neither is it a guide to surface embellishment (embroidery by any other name). Quilting With A Difference is not designed to replace your traditional quilting – but it will provide a few more options to choose from when you've arrived at the quilting stage of your project. I hope you enjoy experimenting with Quilting With A Difference as much as I have and still do!

Nikki Tinkler

Introduction

SOME years ago, I made a big, winter warmer of a quilt entirely out of American flannels which were then new on the market. If you're familiar with this fabric you'll know that, not only is it warm with a brushed pile surface, but it also has quite an open weave, which means that it needs larger-than-usual seam allowances if it's used for patchwork.

Once I'd tacked this particular quilt, the pile of the fabric and its open-weave consistency led to it sitting on the sidelines for a number of weeks (and eventually months) while I thought about how I would quilt it. Being an inveterate lover of hand quilting, I chose not to compromise by machine quilting, even though this would have been the most obvious option at that time (the newly-discovered vermicelli or stipple quilting was densely covering most quilts in exhibitions from head to toe and back again). I was sure that the answer would come if I left the quilt in a prominent position to nag away at me. The temptation to pop it into the nearest cupboard for a few weeks (thereby transforming it into my latest UFO) was great, but thankfully I resisted.

With my thinking cap duly fitted, and with the quilt in a strategic place where it couldn't be ignored, some ideas began filtering through. Going back to basics, I remembered not to try using a fine thread and a small quilting needle on a thick fabric; I began experiments using thicker threads of varying fibres.

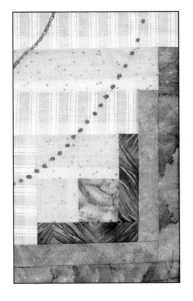

One problem persisted: the basic 'running stitch' appearance of traditional quilting soon disappeared in the raised fabric pile. I therefore needed to find stitches with a more solid appearance – stitches that would show up against the fabric pile.

I started to play with stitches that I had used over the years in canvaswork and tapestry (my pre-quilting days), and then fell upon any old embroidery/needlework books that were gathering dust on my bookshelves and those of the local library. At this point, I'd already set myself a target to be met by these 'alternative' stitches: I needed them for actually quilting through three layers, and not just for surface embellishment. Once I'd built up a small library of suitable stitches, I began to use them on various other projects – finer fabrics, wholecloth projects, etc – and that was the beginning of Quilting With A Difference.

I've been demonstrating Quilting With A Difference at quilt shows for a number of years now, and many people who've seen my work have convinced themselves that the stitching is all worked on a sewing-machine. (I don't mind this comment – in fact I take it as a compliment!) Certainly the stitches give an overall appearance of evenness – even more so when they're sewn on a curved line rather than a straight line – but machine-sewn quilting, whether it's simple straight lines or the use of busier stitches or designs, doesn't create the same softly draping quality in the finished project that hand-quilting does.

At the end of the day, it's all right to give yourself licence to play, and it's good to experiment with both machine- and hand-quilting. But if you're happier stitching by hand then do so – treat your quilting as a marathon and not a sprint, and don't be tempted to turn to the machine purely to increase your output. You may find you're then quilting 'for the wrong reasons' – not a good basis for any creative work.

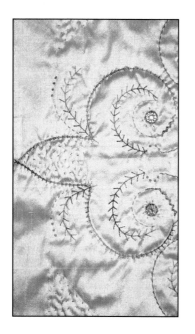

Once you've mastered the stitches that I'll show you, there's nothing stopping you experimenting for yourself – dig out your old needlework books and give other stitches a go. If you're requiring them for actual quilting, try to set yourself the same criteria as I did. You may find that you want to take this technique further and disregard the quilting rules – if so, there's nothing stopping you, though you may have to consider at which point your stitching has stopped being quilting and has become surface embellishment. Basically, quilting is stitching that secures three layers together, but stitches that leave an untidy appearance on the back of your work may be less suitable for a bed quilt or a throw and more suited to a wall-hanging or a cushion, where the back won't be on view so readily.

Remember that if you choose to use some of the busier stitches shown, they'll probably need the visual relief of the plainer stitches alongside them to balance your quilting work. It's quite easy to get carried away with the busier stitches and end up overworking the whole thing. Tread carefully: begin your project with something simple and build up from there. And, above all, enjoy your work – and enjoy the experiments that lead to the finished results, too!

They have gone to make the sunset
Broidered on the western sky
All the colours of our garden
Woven into a lovely curtain
O'er the bed where Day doth lie.

from *The Darkening Garden*
author unknown

The ins and outs of successful sewing

Twists and turns: threads

*In this section we'll explore the different options,
their various uses, how to play with them and
how to look after them*

Types of thread

WHEN you're visiting quilt and craft exhibitions, even if you don't find anything else to buy, treat yourself to a new skein or reel of thread. It's worth building up a collection while you're on your travels, either for use or just for stroking! It's well worth having a delicious collection ready at hand to dip into, perhaps displayed in a special basket or gift box, constantly offering you inspiration and motivation. The colours of contemporary space-dyed threads can themselves often inspire a quilt (without necessarily ever using the thread itself!). And if you've created your project, arrived at the quilting stage and want something just that little bit special to sew with, by the time you've travelled around the countryside in search of the perfect thread your creativity will almost certainly have gone off the boil.

I've experimented with various threads (and still do) for use with my chosen 'alternative' stitches. My collection of threads for quilting now includes not only traditional 100% cotton hand-quilting threads, but also various embroidery threads in cottons, silks and mixed fibres, solid colours, beautiful space-dyed variegated threads, fine crochet cottons and chunky perlés. However, I return time and again to using pure silk thread which passes through the three layers of a quilt beautifully smoothly in comparison with some of the coarser cotton threads.

A selection of threads which I've found suitable for Quilting With A Difference

It's also worth spending time on your invaluable practice 'sandwich' (see opposite) to find a thread that suits you and the fabric that you're working on, and at the same time gives suitable definition to the stitches that you'll be using. Once you've put in all the hard work of quilting, it would be most disappointing to find that your fancier stitches could hardly be seen simply because you'd used an unsuitable fabric or a too-fine thread. Remember: it's possible to use a heavier thread successfully on a fine fabric, but this rarely works the other way round.

Once I began using space-dyed or variegated threads (below), whether cottons or silks, I found interesting things happening with the colour changes. With traditional, 'running stitch' hand-quilting the changes in colour along the stitching line were very subtle, but the busier the stitch I chose to use, the faster the colour change buzzed in and out, adding yet another dimension to my quilting. And if you happen to find the whole hand quilting process a little tedious or (dare I say) boring, this may be your answer – it's amazing how time flies when your eye is caught by constantly changing colours and decorative stitching.

Threads by
Stef Francis

Trying them out

WHICHEVER threads you choose to use, I recommend making and using an experimental practice sandwich – your top fabric layered with your chosen wadding and either backing fabric or butter muslin. (I generally use butter muslin as a backing fabric if I'm quilting a cushion panel, where the back of the work will eventually be hidden inside the cushion cover. Butter muslin is very much an open-weave fabric, though, and may not give you totally accurate results when you're testing out stitches to see how neat – or otherwise! – they'll be when worked through to the back of a quilt.)

Try out all your threads and stitching on your practice piece; you'll be far more experimental and brave on this than you will be on your final, all-important project.

At the same time as you're trying out different stitches, see if the thicker thread that you've chosen enables you to 'pop your knot' as you do when you start and stop in traditional quilting (if you're not sure about this, have a look at the introduction to hand-quilting on page 126). You'll be surprised how thick a thread will still 'pop' – I can even pop the knot with a thick perlé 5. However, if you're worried that the knot-popping will pull or distort the fibres in your top fabric, make an exception in this case, and start and stop your quilting by popping the knot through the fabric on the reverse of your work.

(if you're not sure about this, have a look at the introduction to hand-quilting on page 126)

> If you use a practice piece, it'll make you far braver trying out different stitches and styles.

Do experiment with your threads. I generally stick to single-strand threads, as multiple strands often begin to separate as they're worked through three layers and can create a problem (think: quilting!). Try metallic threads: some will be more fibrous than others, some will be stronger/weaker than others. If you're more adventurous by nature, and especially if you're attending a textile or stitch study course, you might like to try quilting with fine copper wire (see the detail of my quilt *Rainfall at Giverny*, below left) and fine suede thong/strips – I've found both to be successful alternative 'threads'. Again, these are worth collecting while on your travels, and look beautiful displayed in a glass box or a basket while they wait to be used. It's surprising how many reels of metallic threads you'll acquire once friends and family realise that you're collecting them, as they make ideal stocking-fillers or dinner-party gifts …

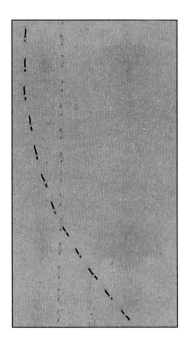

Once you've tried sewing one stitch, perhaps with a fine thread, try the same stitch with a chunkier thread – the end results will vary quite considerably. The sample (opposite) shows the result of working the same stitch (chain stitch) in various different threads – as you can see, some of the threads are notably more successful than others.

Whichever threads you choose to use, remember that when you're quilting with busier stitches, your thread won't last as long as it would with traditional quilting. Therefore, you'll need to thread your needle with a much longer initial length of thread when starting to sew (I sometimes take as much as two arms' length – it soon goes, so don't be tempted to pre-cut your skein as you might for more traditional quilting). Keep an eye on this long length of thread as it works back and forth through all the layers – if the fibres start fraying or thinning, or becoming dull, that particular thread may not be suitable for the project you're working on.

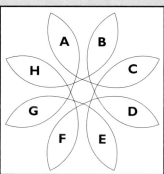

A *Single-strand variegated cotton thread*
Gives excellent stitch definition, but perhaps a little coarse for quilting; can tend to tangle if used in long lengths.

B *Single-strand crochet cotton*
Excellent for quilting, but a little too fine for good stitch definition on busier stitches.

C and **D**
Coton perlé and crochet perlé
Good for big-stitch quilting; a little too thick for the more detailed Quilting With A Difference stitches.

E *Multiple-fibre bouclé yarn*
Asking for trouble! Save yarns like this for couching.

F *Man-made suede-like filament*
Quite weak for quilting through three layers; could be saved for more experimental work.

G *Single-strand variegated 100% silk thread*
Excellent both for quilting and for good stitch definition.

H *Sashiko cotton*
Gives nice definition, but a little too coarse for some of the QWAD stitching – better suited to traditional quilting stitches.

Looking after your threads

TAKE care of your threads both during and after use. If you're working with a skein of thread, a little forward thinking will save you ending up with your thread in a big tangled heap full of knots! Remove the label or labels if there are any when the thread is new and ready to be used. Lay the skein out on the table in front of you and try to unwind it so that it forms one large circle (most skeins are generally folded into a figure of 8). Then you can try either of these options:

a *either* pop this large circle of thread around your neck (warning: avoid dangly earrings, fancy necklaces and spectacle chains – and I would recommend only one skein around your neck at a time!); clip away the knot in the thread to release two raw ends and work from this. (Remember to pull the skein round to the front as you pull the raw end of thread off to one side.)

b *or* wind the skein onto a spare piece of card on an empty cotton reel.

This is not only a good way to use up all those empty cotton reels, it also avoids having piles of knotted threads that just don't have the same appeal, somehow, as a new thread.

Threads that fight back

SOME threads simply will not pass successfully through three layers of a project, or won't go through the top layer of fabric. Chunkies/knobblies/multiple-stranded fibrous fancies: threads that won't pass easily through three layers can always be couched onto the fabric (you see? there's no excuse for not buying it!); refer to the section on couching (see page 67).

Making the change

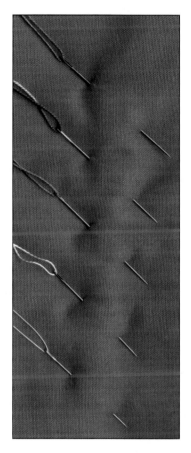

IF you're working with a chunkier thread than you would usually use, you'll almost certainly find that the eye of a quilter's needle (also known as a Quilter's Between) is too small to accommodate this thicker thread. Choose your alternative needle carefully; if you're used to using Betweens, you'll already know that they are quite rigid compared with embroidery needles, and it can take a while to adjust your stitching technique.

I find that I can quilt successfully with any needle taken from a mixed pack of embroidery needles in sizes 5-10. Each of these has an eye large enough to accommodate a slightly-thicker-than-normal quilting thread – although a pure silk thread will usually prove an easier option than a cotton one. If you have trouble threading this size of needle, try buying a mixed pack of household needles and find one that suits you. The whippier shank on these alternative needles may mean that it will eventually bend and may even break at some stage, but you have to do a fair amount of intense quilting before that happens – and even the best Betweens have been known to break under pressure eventually.

The temptation at this stage can be to move towards using a thicker-shanked embroidery needle. The problem with the thicker shank will soon show up in your quilting – it's quite difficult to quilt through three layers with a thicker-shanked needle *and* a thicker thread. Quilting should be enjoyable, and not hard work – if your fingers become sore from forcing the needle through your quilt project you need to reassess the needle you're using. Try to find and use a larger-eyed, sharp-pointed needle with not too thick a shank. Basically, the needle needs to produce a hole in the fabric that is large enough for the thread to pass through, but no larger.

Also, have a blunt tapestry needle available; this is useful if you're going to do a large amount of whipping or threading under previous stitches, where you need to avoid catching unwanted threads and fabric fibres with the point of your needle. If you're only doing a small amount of whipping and/or threading, you may find you can get away with just turning your needle back to front and passing the eye of the needle under the previous stitches (be careful of pushing on the pointed end of the needle though!)

Pain or pleasure? Thimbles

On my travels while teaching and demonstrating, I have a lot of discussions with fellow quiltmakers about thimbles.

Different types of thimble

IF you use a metal thimble and have been happily using one for years, then carry on – you do not have a problem (but see the note below). Many needleworkers, however, find metal thimbles difficult to use. The metal thimble, with its dimpled surface, was primarily designed for quilters who work in a frame; when quilting with your work in a frame or a hoop, the eye of the needle is intended to rest in the dimples of the thimble while the finger alone rocks the needle up and down in the work (see page 127). Dimpled metal thimbles are not truly designed for those of us quilters who like to lap quilt (without a hoop or frame), which necessitates gripping the needle between finger and thumb.

When I first began quilting (with metallic thimble and *sans* hoop), I noticed that at the point where I gripped the needle, the thimble rubbed the thread against the eye of the needle while I was stitching and weakened the thread, often to breaking point. (Not so bad on the outside of the work where it could be rectified, but it was quite worrying to think of that weakened thread *inside* a quilt.) I began to experiment with alternative thimbles. At that time, fingerwrap thimbles were available – an American product which seems to have disappeared from our shops. (I've now found a source of almost the same type of 'fabric' and can supply these to anyone wishing to try them – see page 143). I find them excellent for a variety of reasons, not least as an introduction to wearing something on your finger (large amounts of hand quilting without covering your needle-pushing digit is an unnecessarily unpleasant and painful experience, and quilting, after all, is not meant to be a blood sport!) Also, this is a good, inexpensive thimble to take to workshops and quilting group days.

From the fingerwrap thimble, I moved on to soft leather thimbles; there are a number of these available on the British market at the moment, most of which incorporate a metal disc at the pushing point. The soft leather enables lap quilters actually to feel the needle when gripping it between finger and thumb – the metal disc provides the extra strength required when pushing the needle through the three layers. (Any quilter worth their salt knows that excruciating feeling when the needle penetrates the skin on the top of the pushing finger – to be avoided at all costs!) There is also a longer version of the soft leather thimble which incorporates an elasticated fabric panel on one side, and which covers the finger down its length and past the second knuckle joint – this can be more comfortable for arthritic finger joints which don't accommodate shorter thimbles or metal thimbles comfortably.

Undercover story

THERE are also products available which are designed to protect your 'underneath' finger – the one that feels the point of the needle when it protrudes from the back of the work and guides the needle point back in. Again, a metal or solid thimble doesn't allow you to feel the needle

point at this stage, and anything made of fabric would inevitably end up being stitched to the back of your project! Finger protection discs are available from good patchwork and quilting suppliers. Also worth trying is a layer of skin protection cream (available from your local pharmacy or camping shop), as used by walkers to form a thin protective barrier over areas prone to blisters.

The cutting edge: scissors and rotary equipment

Scissors

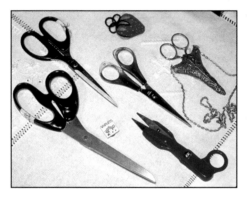

THE chances are that you have already armed yourself with a large pair of fabric-cutting shears, possibly a medium-sized pair of sharp scissors and some scissors that are kept purely for cutting paper and/or card. Do also invest in a pair of small, sharp embroidery scissors – they don't have to be expensive. It's a false economy to try to snip thread close to the fabric surface with a huge pair of fabric-cutting shears. I've seen this happen often (along with the dubious use of teeth!) – you'll invariably snip your fabric by mistake sometime, and that can be very demoralising.

Rotary cutters

Always keep the blade of your rotary cutter sharp; it's safer than using a blunt blade.

ROTARY cutting equipment certainly speeds up the process when constructing your quilt. Even if you prefer to use templates for your patchwork, once your fabric has been marked up and is ready to cut, if the different shapes have been aligned in fairly straight rows it's then a comparatively quick job just to rotary cut between the shapes. You'll also find that the fabric will distort less, as it is not being lifted and handled so much.

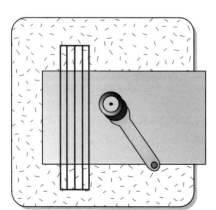

Rotary cutters come in various shapes and sizes, and so do the self-healing cutting mats that you use with them. Keep the blades of your rotary cutters very sharp; they'll cut the fabric more efficiently, and you won't need to press so hard, which means that the cutter is less likely to slip. You can buy tools for sharpening rotary cutter blades, but sometimes it can be less trouble simply to change to a new, sharp blade (you can keep your old, used blades safely stored and labelled separately for using on paper). The main thing to remember when working with a rotary cutter is to keep the blade covered whenever you're not using it; get into the habit of slipping the safety cover over the blade every time you put the tool down. Some cutters cover the blade automatically when there's no pressure on the handle.

And do invest in a special rotary-cutting safety ruler at the same time. These are quite thick and made of toughened acrylic, and they're designed to keep your fingers away from the cutting blade. They're marked up with all sorts of grids, designed to help you square up your fabric even when cutting on the bias.

Making your mark: fabric marking tools and tips

Everyone has their favourite way of marking the fabric ready for quilting, but don't be afraid to try out different methods for different projects

Types of marking tool

IT'S handy to build up a collection of different fabric markers – don't expect to buy one marking tool and hope that it will work on all the fabrics that you will ever buy or use. A good starting point is to buy a white pencil for dark/busy fabrics (I find that an artist's watercolour pencil works well for marking most types of fabric), and a quilter's silver pencil for lighter fabrics. I find that my white artist's pencil will show up on even the palest pastels and I tend to use that more than anything, taking a darker marking pen or pencil as a last resort.

> Keep a dry face flannel in your workroom. Gently rub it over areas of quilting to remove soft/chalky markings left on the fabric surface. (This cloth also works well for removing threads trapped in your rotary cutting board; wipe it over the board in a circular motion.)

Other fabric marking equipment that I've collected over the years includes both tailor's chalk and chalk wheels (really only useful as a temporary mark-maker and not advisable for intricate patterns); a soapstone pencil (these can be bought from most patchwork and quilting shops); both blue water-soluble and purple air-soluble pens; and specialised quilter's lead pencils. Alongside these, I also keep a stock of quilter's masking tape (a useful quarter-inch tape which enables you to sew alongside it and then remove it, thereby avoiding marking the fabric at all). It's as well to remember that the sharp point of a needle or pin (or a special plastic marker which looks like a shirt-collar point prodder), run along the surface of fabric, will make a fairly permanent mark which can be used for a quilting design.

Whichever tool or technique you choose, you'll find that the busier stitches used in Quilting With A Difference will generally cover up your marked lines, and so their removal will be less of a worry than with traditional quilting – another bonus!

Water-soluble fabric-marking pens

THESE pens generally create a turquoise-blue line, though some water-soluble pens also produce a purple or pink line. There has been a lot of discussion in quilting circles in recent years about the dubious use of the chemicals that these pens contain. Certainly, they should be used with caution. I have an early quilt which shows very clearly the end result of leaving blue pen in fabric over a few years without washing it out; it has caused a bleached-out area in a navy fabric. I've also seen a similar process in a paler green fabric; here the line reappeared as pale brown. Having said that, I still keep water-soluble pens in my fabric-marking collection – if used with care and caution (the key words) they can be an invaluable addition to your collection.

TIPS

These tips will help you to get the best results from this kind of marking pen. Buy the finest-tipped pen that you can. When marking your fabric, don't be tempted to press too hard on the surface of the fabric – and don't go back and forth to produce a strong ink line; one soft line will be enough. Given a few patient seconds the ink line will show up and be sufficiently visible for you to follow when stitching your design.

> Water-soluble pen marks must always be removed with cold water; heat will set the ink permanently.

Very fine marking pen liners have such a small felt tip that they hold very little ink at any one time. Bearing this in mind, don't be tempted to throw away your fine liner if it doesn't work quickly enough – try keeping two and using them in tandem while marking up your project, thereby giving each one time to recharge itself. The lines made by these pens are water-soluble, but it's vital to remember that heat will set the ink. So, once the fabric is marked, don't iron the project, and don't leave it lying in sunlight or close to a heat source.

When washing out the ink line, use *cold* water, and not hot. I find that if I've only drawn a sufficiently fine line with my pen, and not soaked the fabric with the ink, a barely damp cotton wool bud just blotted across the marked line is enough to remove it.

If you prefer to use a thicker blue pen, you're going to make a very strong mark on your fabric with a lot of ink – this means that your project will need to be immersed in (cold!) water to remove all of the ink residue. If you just try to blot out the marked line you'll invariably end up with tide marks of ink appearing on your fabric surface, arising from the ink floating around in the wadding and coming back up in odd and unwanted places. Remember: caution is the word.

Air-soluble fabric-marking pens

THESE pens generally create purple or pink lines on the fabric, which gently fade without needing to be sponged out. The pink air-soluble pens can usually be found among the dressmakers' equipment of haberdashery departments, whereas patchwork and quilting retailers tend to stock the purple versions, which often show up a little more strongly.

The accompanying instruction sheet will tell you that the pen mark will stay visible for a day or so. In my experience, the purple pen (again, using only the very fine version, and used with care and caution as described above) will provide a very temporary mark to follow. I've used this marker successfully in past quilts, but only for sewing short, straight lines. I will thread my needle, draw in my quilting line and begin to sew – generally the mark will have almost disappeared before I reach the end of my stitching. If any pen mark is still visible, these pens are also water-soluble, so again a barely damp cotton wool bud will dampen the fabric enough to remove the marked line.

Inevitably, these pens contain chemicals that you may or may not want to use in your quilts. I can only go by experience – the earlier quilts on which I used air-soluble pens are showing no detrimental effect as yet. I'll keep you posted! (And if you are concerned about using chemicals on your fabric, then perhaps ordinary lead pencils should be used with some caution too.)

Warp and weft: choosing suitable fabrics

Selecting the right fabrics is one key to a successful finished project

Pick your focus

WHEN you're choosing your fabrics for a quilt, just as when you're planning its original design, you need to bear in mind the project as a whole. Do you want your eye to be drawn to the stitching itself? If so, choose a thread and fabric which will contrast well with each other (this contrast can be subtle or strong) and possibly some fancier stitches. If you would prefer your eye to be drawn to the puffs and pillows of the quilting design itself, then aim for a thread which is a fairly close match to the colour of your fabric, or even a shade darker, and simpler stitching.

Below left: plain fabrics and those with small prints work best with QWAD stitches

Below right: never say 'never,' but … fabrics with large or novelty prints don't make very good backgrounds for QWAD designs

Some of the more complex stitches in this book will show up even on a fairly busy print. However, you don't have to plump for a plain fabric if you want your design to be obvious – you can choose a print that reads as a plain (ie a marble or small overall print – see below left). I would advise against stitching decorative work (or, for that matter, any intricate hand-quilting) on a loud, in-your-face print (see below right) – the amount of time spent on your quilting will almost be a waste if it can't ultimately be seen.

Fabrics loaned by Puddleducks

Dupion silks from The Silk Route

I've used dress-weight dupion silks equally successfully for both patchwork and quilting. Dupion silk has a slight texture provided by the slub; it's also a fairly stable silk and doesn't have the slippery, hard-to-handle tendencies of many finer silks. This stability means that it rarely creases and makes it excellent for patchwork piecing, although you should work with a slightly larger seam allowance to allow for the fabric fraying somewhat more than most cottons. I've also successfully machine washed a quilt containing a mix of pure cotton fabrics and dupion silk. The silk will inevitably lose some of its sheen and stability when washed, though, so it's probably best to have pieces containing silk dry-cleaned.

Fabric preparation

THE pre-washing of patchwork and quilting fabrics is always an open debate among quiltmakers. For every dozen quilters who pre-wash their fabrics, there will be a dozen who choose not to. Which is what it boils down to: choice. Most fabric retailers will advise you to pre-wash all fabrics just in case any colour run or shrinkage occurs – obviously, with many hundreds of thousands of bolts of fabric on their shelves, it's not feasible for them to test swatches of all the cloth that passes through their hands. The same may be said about manufacturers' recommend-ations – although we would hope that certain colour and shrinkage testing had been done before the fabric had reached the retail outlet, this isn't always the case. (Interestingly, I've recently come across this manufacturer's recommendation, attached to a new bolt of fabric: '… do not pre-wash prior to using. The fabric … must be a specific size. Once the fabric has been sewn into the quilt and quilted, it will be stabilized, and then can be laundered.' An interesting slant on an old chestnut.)

Personally, I choose not to pre-wash my patchwork or quilt fabrics *in most cases*. I like the feel of a new fabric, and once it's been washed, even with a nice steam iron and the addition of spray or wash-in starch, for me it's lost its allure and become 'old' or 'used' (and I certainly wouldn't want to have all my dupion silk dry-cleaned before using it!) I would make an exception if the project I was working on was due to be excessively machine laundered and manhandled. I feel you have to treat each quilt project independently as it comes along, and make suitable decisions for each different quilt.

The inside story: waddings

We have more choice than ever of what goes inside our quilts;
how do we choose the 'filling' for our 'sandwich'?

Types of wadding

THERE are numerous waddings on the market these days – quilters are quite spoilt for choice. Some of the many types available are shown in the photographs opposite; the qualities of the different waddings shown are described in the key below. The only wadding that gives a fair amount of loft (ie thickness and fluffiness) is a 2oz polyester, and there's no reason why you shouldn't use it (don't be tempted to go for a heavier weight – 2oz is ample to stitch through when you're quilting by hand). There are a number of bleached and unbleached pure cotton waddings on the market (although not all of these will be suitable for hand-quilting), together with mixed fibre waddings, silks, woollens, even lambswool.

My favourite wadding at the moment is a mix of 80% cotton, 20% polyester. As always, try to accumulate a selection of sample pieces, or at least a small page of notes listing the different waddings and their properties/suitability for hand or machine work; you can keep this in your handbag when you're shopping. Each project that you work on needs to be thought about individually, and your waddings/threads/fabrics etc chosen accordingly. Think, too, about how much more you want to spend on your project at the wadding stage – and do you mind pre-washing your wadding? All these things will have a bearing on your final choice.

A 2oz polyester; an inexpensive wadding which gives generous loft to the finished project. Washes well, but will go completely flat if ironed. Available in heavier weights, but 2oz is generally used for hand-quilting; doesn't require pre-washing.

B 2oz polyester as above, in charcoal grey.

C 100% wool; suitable for quilting by hand or machine. Provides higher degree of insulation than polyester. Check manufacturers' recommendations for pre-washing.

D 100% compressed polyester; a very flat wadding with some insulation, suitable for tableware, wall-hangings etc. Only suitable for quilts if you want a very flat result. Can be difficult to hand-quilt, but ideal for machine-quilting.

E 60% Australian wool/40% polyester; a distinctive wadding with good insulation. Excellent for quilting, and does not require pre-washing: moth-proofed!

F 100% cotton; comes as natural and bleached with varying levels of loft. A natural-fibre wadding; there are a number of different makes on the market; avoid ones with scrim if you're hand-quilting. A certain amount of shrinkage means optional pre-washing.

G 80% cotton/20% polyester; produces a small amount of shrinkage so pre-washing is optional. Excellent for hand-quilting and machining.

H British lambswool; beautifully soft – a shame to hide it inside a quilt! High insulation properties, good loft, suitable for quilted wearables; a little tricky if you want to hand-quilt.

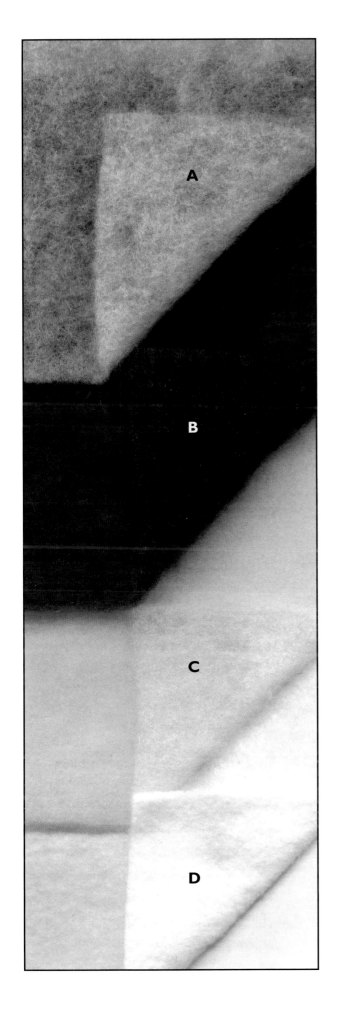

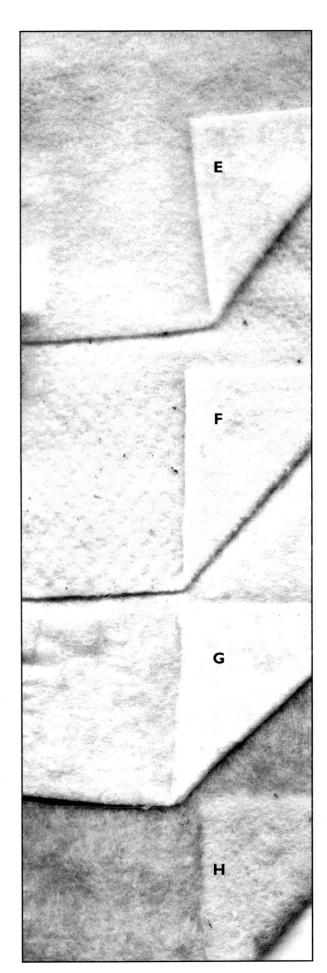

Quilting in a nutshell

THINGS to consider before quilting your project:

- Does the design of your quilt suit the three-layer method of construction, or quilt-as-you-go?
- Consider the fibre content and print design of your fabrics, back and front
- Do you want to work a wholecloth quilt or a patchwork (pieced) project?
- Choose your wadding carefully to suit your method of quilting and the desired end result
- Give some thought to your design and style of quilting: traditional or contemporary patterns – traced/stencilled/drawn freehand – traditional or QWAD stitching, or a mixture of both?
- Choose your fabric marking tools and decide whether you're marking up before or after layering your quilt
- Select your threads to suit your fabric and your design
- Choose your needles carefully, and try not to work without a thimble

Looking after yourself

Your health, comfort and safety must be a consideration when quilting

If you experience pain in either your hands, wrist, arms or shoulder during or after quilting, reassess your chosen quilting technique. Hand-quilting can set up a certain amount of tension throughout the hand and arm; if you have a problem, try sewing with your work in a hoop. You could also try a support glove, available from quilting specialists. If you do have a problem, don't leave it unattended; it won't go away, and might well become more serious! If you haven't done so already, try adding machine-quilting to your repertoire to provide more options.

The height at which you work, along with your posture and tension while sewing, can all contribute to health problems, but many of these can be averted. Relieve stress in your lower back and shoulder area simply by lowering your seat in relation to your work table while you're using the sewing machine, and raise the height of your cutting table – easier to do if you have a typist's chair and/or a table with adjustable-height legs. When you're lap-quilting, one or two pillows or cushions on your lap, underneath the piece to be stitched, will raise the work nearer to your eye-level, and you'll avoid straining your whole back and neck area downwards towards the work in your lap.

let's get stitching
now it's time for you to try
Quilting With A Difference

Rock-bound weed sways out and in,
Coral-red and bottle-green.
Wondrous pale anemones
Stir like flowers in a breeze ...

from *The Pool in the Rock*
by Walter de la Mare

Choosing your stitches

Picking the best stitches for your quilt is another key to success

Narrowing the field ...

IN theory, many different stitches can be used for quilting; in practice, some prove much more successful than others. Here are my personal criteria for choosing new stitches to use in my work.

> You'll find it easier to lap quilt with QWAD stitching, rather than using a hoop – but the choice is yours.

a Any 'new' stitch has to be suitable for quilting through three layers (not as straightforward as it may sound, as you'll soon discover when you begin to work on your own experimental sampler).

b I want to be able to sew the stitch with some fluidity – ie I don't want it to take very much more time, if any, than my traditional hand-quilting would.

c I have to be able to work the stitches from the front or surface of the work only. (The temptation here is to begin to stab-stitch the embroidery stitches, ie to pass the needle through to the back of the work, pull all the thread through to the back and then bring the needle back through the work to the front. Not only is this time-consuming, but you won't achieve a neat appearance on the back of your project – as anyone who has tried stab-stitching traditional quilting will have discovered.)

d As I don't generally quilt with a frame or a quilting hoop, I avoid stitches that would usually rely on stretching in an embroidery ring. Although Quilting With A Difference can be used successfully by quilters who use a hoop, I've found that most quilters will discard their hoop quite early on in favour of lap quilting.

e I've discarded a lot of the stitches that I've experimented with as unsuitable – for me – as they give an untidy appearance to the back of the work. (Remember, I need stitches for quilting a quilt, and that means a bed quilt as well as a wall-hanging.)

f The final result has to provide some textural interest to the surface of the project.

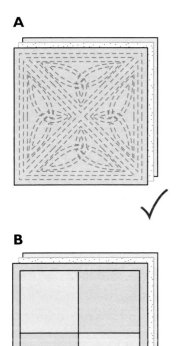

A

B

C

Remember that not all projects will either need or benefit from these stitches. Wholecloth quilts (**A**) work well, and so do many simple pieced quilt tops (**B**). If you have worked some intricate, pieced patchwork or appliqué within your project (**C**), or if you've used a bold and loud printed fabric, then it will probably be better to stick with traditional quilt stitches that won't detract from the work – it's advisable to treat each project individually and on its own merit when you come to the quilting stage.

None of the stitches in this book have been invented by me out of malice – they are all traditional embroidery stitches to be found in any good embroidery book. I've also kept in mind their use for sewing traditional quilting designs. They can, of course, be played and experimented with and altered to suit yourself so, if you're one of the more adventurous souls among us, try lengthening, shortening, widening, overlapping these given stitches and possibly others that you may find – the options are endless. Don't forget, though, that quiltmakers should always bear in mind what's happening on the reverse side of their project …

Practice makes perfect

THE more you use these stitches, the more even and pleasing they will become – as with so many crafts, it really is a case of practice makes perfect. Do bear in mind, though, that it's a little like hand-knitting – when you first pick up your work, it may take some time for the tension and rhythm to regulate themselves. It's wise, therefore, to keep a practice fabric 'sandwich' by your project to work on before you move back to the *pièce de resistance*. (Many years ago, professional travelling quilters would do just this so that they could regulate their stitching before sewing on the commissioned quilt.) Also, with some of the busier stitches you'll find that it's more difficult to achieve an even appearance when they're worked on a straight line, but they give a very even overall appearance when worked on a curved line. This is a welcome optical illusion, and can be used to great effect with many traditional quilting designs such as cable and rope designs, fleur de lys, hearts and feathers (see examples on pages 99 and 107).

I strongly recommend that you make your own practice fabric 'sandwich'; this can be as basic as you like or as time permits. However, if you'd prefer to keep a more attractive and practical record of your stitch experiments, look at the diagrams on pages 77-79 showing alternative designs for suitable stitch samplers. These provide an excellent way of trying out new stitches while also resulting in an attractive wallhanging; you'll also have a permanent reminder of which stitches you prefer – and those you don't!

Choosing your designs

Select quilting designs that complement your stitches

Stretching the boundaries

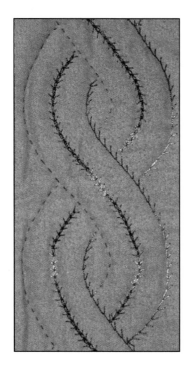

WHEN I began experimenting with Quilting With A Difference, I set myself the boundary of using embroidery stitches within somewhat restrained, traditional quilting designs; beginning this way helped me to focus on what I was trying to achieve with the stitches themselves. Initially I chose familiar cabled and feathered designs, and then continued with commercial quilting stencils – I felt that I was making the alternative stitches become recognised quilting stitches by working within these set boundaries.

Once I'd settled in my own mind that the QWAD technique worked with traditional designs, I began to try more stylised and freehand drawn designs. It's possible to use this technique in quite a free and liberated way while still adhering to my initial 'rules' of quilting (not necessarily the same criteria as everyone else's). So, if you're wondering what your starting point should be for your quilting designs, work with whatever style you have felt most comfortable with in your previous quilting projects.

a

If you tend to prefer traditional designs (**a**), take a look at the vast range of specialist quilting stencils available through patchwork and quilting retail outlets and mail order catalogues, perhaps choosing a design that both appeals to you and also gives you scope for experimental stitching. If you like to work more individually, you could draw a quarter of your design onto dressmakers' gridded paper (**b**); you can then use repeats of the design to create a nicely symmetrical pattern (**c**). Or you might simply prefer to draw a stylised design completely freehand straight onto your fabric – the design doesn't necessarily have to be symmetrical (**d**). The choice is yours. In any case, I find that it is nice to have some sort of a marked line to follow – this allows you to concentrate on your stitches and not on where your design is going.

The perfect partnership

ONCE you've chosen your basic design, you'll need to consider how close the lines of the pattern lie alongside each other. If there are lines that pass very close to each other (**e**), almost butting up, this will limit the stitches that you can choose for that particular section of the design – for instance, you'll probably have to choose narrower stitches, such as coral stitch or chain stitch, for both of these lines, rather than wider stitches such as herringbone or wheatear stitch. This in turn may dictate the stitches that you use for any larger areas that evolve from this small section. You just need to think ahead a little and take a good look at the design (not only as a whole, but also the smaller individual sections) before you begin stitching.

If there are areas within your quilting design that look a little bland or bare (**f**), think about using filling stitches (**g**) – see pages 68-72 for details and ideas. I've used seeding successfully to fill different areas on a number of quilts. You can also think about adding beads in different ways (see page 73), and using shisha (little mirrors – see pages 74-76).

The Stitches

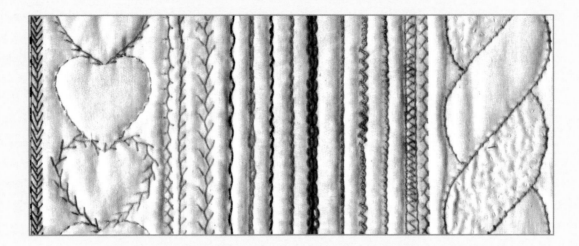

In this section you'll find a whole range of different stitches that I've tried out and which I feel work well for Quilting with a Difference.

Each stitch has illustrations and instructions for both right-handed and left-handed needleworkers; remember to follow the correct sequence!

RIGHT-HANDED

LEFT-HANDED

Stitches featured:

running stitch	zigzag chain stitch	Vandyke stitch
threaded running stitch	half feather stitch	wheatear stitch
whipped running stitch	single feather stitch	long-armed cross stitch
chain stitch	fly stitch	open Cretan stitch
threaded chain stitch	fern stitch	coral stitch
whipped chain stitch	blanket stitch	sword-edged stitch
open chain stitch	closed blanket stitch	chevron stitch
	herringbone stitch	double knot stitch

Running stitch

RIGHT-HANDED

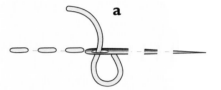

LEFT-HANDED

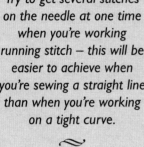

• STITCHING TIP •

Try to get several stitches on the needle at one time when you're working running stitch – this will be easier to achieve when you're sewing a straight line than when you're working on a tight curve.

Bring the needle to the surface at the right-hand end of your stitching line. Working from right to left, take a series of small, even stitches through the fabric. Make the stitches at even intervals, whether you're working along a straight line (**a**) or a curved one (**b**).

Bring the needle to the surface at the left-hand end of your stitching line. Working from left to right, take a series of small, even stitches through the fabric. Make the stitches at even intervals, whether you're working along a straight line (**a**) or a curved one (**b**).

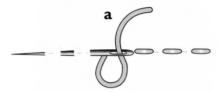

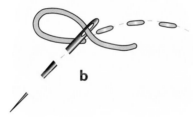

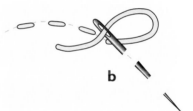

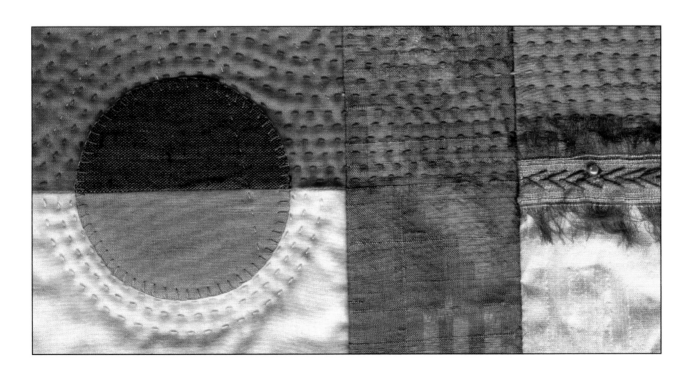

Threaded running stitch

 RIGHT-HANDED

Working from the right-hand end of your stitching line, bring the needle out so that it emerges under the first running stitch. Weave your needle down through the next stitch, up through the following one and so on along the line (**a**). The contrasting thread will form loops between the first stitches. These can be left fairly loose if the project is to be a decorative wall-hanging, but need to be pulled fairly taut for use on a quilt so that they don't snag.

If you wish, you can thread the stitches again with a second yarn, perhaps in a third colour, this time going up through the stitches you have previously threaded downwards and so on (**b**).

 LEFT-HANDED

Working from the left-hand end of your stitching line, bring the needle out so that it emerges under the first running stitch. Weave your needle down through the next stitch, up through the following one and so on along the line (**a**). The contrasting thread will form loops between the first stitches. These can be left fairly loose if the project is to be a decorative wall-hanging, but need to be pulled fairly taut for use on a quilt so that they don't snag.

If you wish, you can thread the stitches again with a second yarn, perhaps in a contrasting colour, this time going up through the stitches you have previously threaded downwards and so on (**b**).

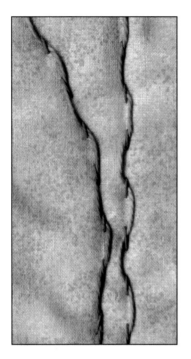

> ## • STITCHING TIP •
>
> *When you're using variegated threads to whip or thread existing stitches, inevitably the colour will have changed as you come round the second time. This effect is part of the charm of using variegated threads; there's no need to change your thread unless you particularly want to.*

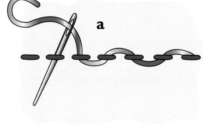

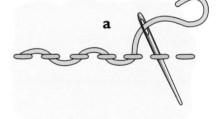

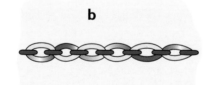

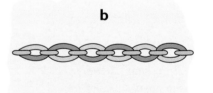

Threaded running stitch on a curved line

Whipped running stitch

RIGHT-HANDED

LEFT-HANDED

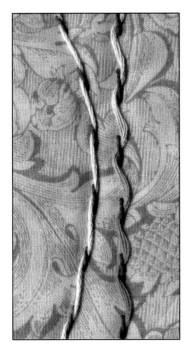

Working from the right-hand end of your stitching line, bring the needle out so that it emerges under the first running stitch. Take your needle down through each running stitch in turn, making sure that you don't catch the fabric or the original stitches (**a**).

For an extra-strong line, whip the stitches once from right to left and then work back in the other direction with a second thread (**b**).

Working from the left-hand end of your stitching line, bring the needle out so that it emerges under the first running stitch. Take your needle down through each running stitch in turn, making sure that you don't catch the fabric or the original stitches (**a**).

For an extra-strong line, whip the stitches once from left to right and then work back in the other direction with a second thread (**b**).

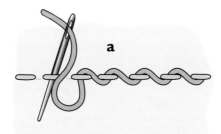

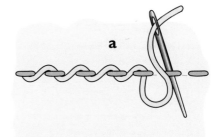

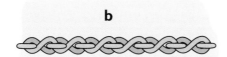

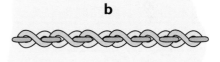

• STITCHING TIP •

When you're whipping and threading stitches, it's easiest to use a blunt tapestry needle to ensure that you don't catch the original stitches or the fabric with your needle-tip. An alternative, if you don't want to change needles, is to turn your ordinary sewing needle around and push it eye-first under your existing stitches.

Whipped running stitch on a curved line

~ Chain stitch ~

 RIGHT-HANDED

 LEFT-HANDED

RIGHT-HANDED

Bring the thread out on your stitching line. Insert the needle at the end of your stitching line, where the thread emerges, and bring it out a short way further along the line, allowing the thread to loop under the needle tip (**a**).

Pull the thread through to form the first link, then form the second loop in the same way, inserting the needle where the thread emerges inside the first link (**b**).

When your line of stitching is complete, secure the final loop with a tiny straight stitch (**c**).

LEFT-HANDED

Bring the thread out on your stitching line. Insert the needle at the end of your stitching line, where the thread emerges, and bring it out a short way further along the line, allowing the thread to loop under the needle tip (**a**).

Pull the thread through to form the first link, then form the second loop in the same way, inserting the needle where the thread emerges inside the first link (**b**).

When your line of stitching is complete, secure the final loop with a tiny straight stitch (**c**).

> **• STITCHING TIP •**
>
> *You'll find it time-consuming to take a stitch and then stop to wrap the thread round the needle. Instead, hold the thread forward along the stitching line, forming a loop for the needle tip to emerge inside.*
>
> ~

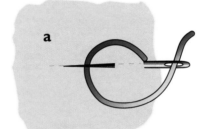

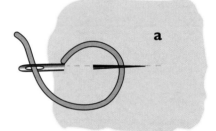

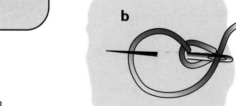

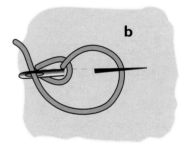

Chain stitch on a curved line

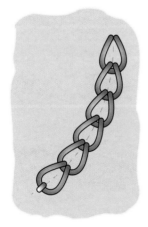

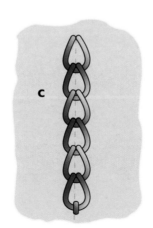

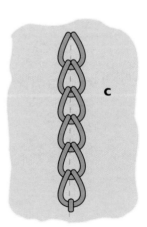

Threaded chain stitch

RIGHT-HANDED

Working from the right-hand end of your stitching line, bring the needle out so that it emerges just beyond the first link of the chain. Weave your needle down through the first link, up through the following one and so on along the line (**a**), making sure that you don't catch the fabric or the original stitches.

At the end of the chain, take the threading stitch down through the fabric to finish it off (**b**).

If you wish you can work a second line of threading, perhaps with a contrasting colour, this time going up through the links you have previously threaded downwards and so on (**c**). This creates a very strong cable effect (**d**).

LEFT-HANDED

Working from the left-hand end of your stitching line, bring the needle out so that it emerges just beyond the first link of the chain. Weave your needle down through the first link, up through the following one and so on along the line (**a**), making sure that you don't catch the fabric or the original stitches.

At the end of the chain, take the threading stitch down through the fabric to finish it off (**b**).

If you wish you can work a second line of threading, perhaps with a contrasting colour, this time going up through the links you have previously threaded downwards and so on (**c**). This creates a very strong cable effect (**d**).

• STITCHING TIP •

If you're going to thread chain stitch, use a much chunkier yarn for the threading than you used for the original stitches. Finer threads, or even those of the same thickness, have a tendency to disappear when they're pulled quite tight – which you need to do when you're using this stitch for quilting.

If you use a similar-weight thread for threading, it will appear as flashes of colour between the links, so use a contrasting colour or shade for the best effect.

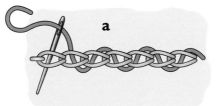
a

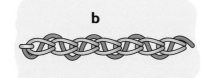
b

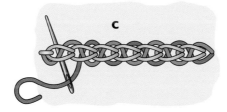
c

d

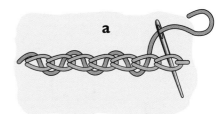
a

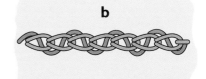
b

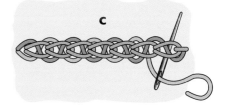
c

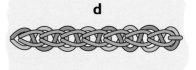
d

Whipped chain stitch

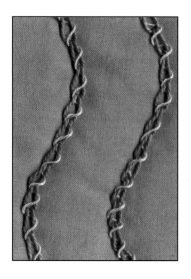

RIGHT-HANDED

Working from the right-hand end of your stitching line, bring the needle out so that it emerges just beyond the first chain stitch. Take your needle down behind each stitched link of the 'chain' in turn, making sure that you don't catch the fabric or the original stitches (**a**).

Thread each link in the same way, then take the needle down through the fabric at the end of the stitching line (**b**).

For variety, try whipping the stitches once downwards, then work upwards through each link with a second thread (**c**); this creates a strong stitching line (**d**).

LEFT-HANDED

Working from the left-hand end of your stitching line, bring the needle out so that it emerges just beyond the first chain stitch. Take your needle down behind each stitched link of the 'chain' in turn, making sure that you don't catch the fabric or the original stitches (**a**).

Thread each link in the same way, then take the needle down through the fabric at the end of the stitching line (**b**).

For variety, try whipping the stitches once downwards, then work upwards through each link with a second thread (**c**); this creates a strong stitching line (**d**).

• STITCHING TIP •

Try whipping your chain stitch with a fine metallic thread – the result will be a very subtle twinkle added to your work.

a
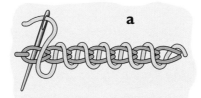

b
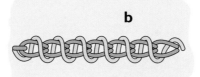

c
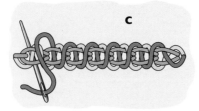

d

a
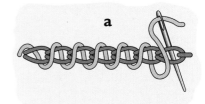

b
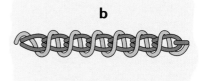

c
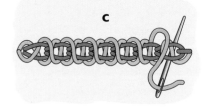

d
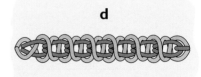

∼ *Open chain stitch* ∼

 RIGHT-HANDED

Begin to the left of your stitching line, and insert the needle to the right of the stitching line at the same level. Insert the needle diagonally so that the tip emerges below and to the left as shown, allowing the thread to loop under the needle tip (**a**).

Pull the thread through gently, leaving a slightly loose link, then insert the needle in the right-hand edge of the first link to secure it as shown (**b**).

Continue stitching links in the same way, keeping them even in width; finish off the final link of your stitching line with two little straight stitches, one at each side (**c**).

 LEFT-HANDED

Begin to the right of your stitching line, and insert the needle to the left of the stitching line at the same level. Insert the needle diagonally so that the tip emerges below and to the right as shown, allowing the thread to loop under the needle tip (**a**).

Pull the thread through gently, leaving a slightly loose link, then insert the needle in the left-hand edge of the first link to secure it as shown (**b**).

Continue stitching links in the same way, keeping them even in width; finish off the final link of your stitching line with two little straight stitches, one at each side (**c**).

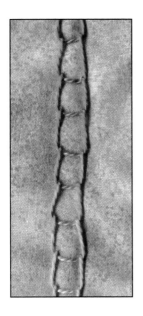

• STITCHING TIP •

Make sure that you leave the loop of each link slightly loose, so that you have room to insert the needle ready for the next link. If you pull the link too tight, it won't be loose enough to spread widthways to form the little box shape.

∼

Open chain stitch on a curved line

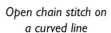

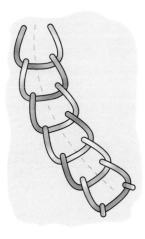

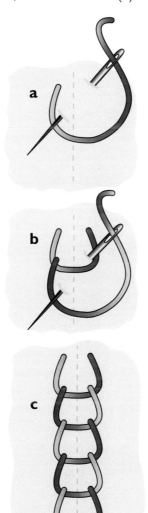

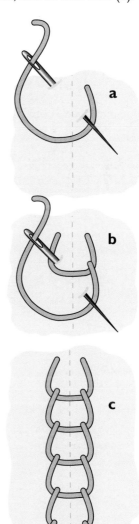

~ Zigzag chain stitch ~

 RIGHT-HANDED

Begin at the right-hand edge of your stitching line, and bring your thread out just below the line. Insert the needle where the thread emerges, and bring it out a short way to the left and just above the stitching line, allowing the thread to loop under the needle tip (**a**).

Pull the thread through to form the first link, then insert the needle just to the left of where the thread emerges so that it pierces the thread of the first link. Form the second loop in the same way but this time with the needle emerging to the left and below the stitching line (**b**).

When your line of stitching is complete, secure the final loop with a tiny straight stitch (**c**).

 LEFT-HANDED

Begin at the left-hand edge of your stitching line, and bring your thread out just below the line. Insert the needle where the thread emerges, and bring it out a short way to the right and just above the stitching line, allowing the thread to loop under the needle tip (**a**).

Pull the thread through to form the first link, then insert the needle just to the right of where the thread emerges so that it pierces the thread of the first link. Form the second loop in the same way but this time with the needle emerging to the right and below the stitching line (**b**).

When your line of stitching is complete, secure the final loop with a tiny straight stitch (**c**).

• STITCHING TIP •

Do take the time to pierce the thread of the previous chain with the point of your needle; if you don't, you'll find that your zigzag chains will eventually roll inwards. Take sharp angles, too — otherwise the stitching line will flatten out too much, and look like a slightly uneven chain stitch.

~

a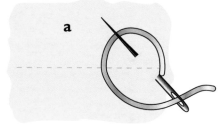

a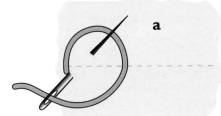

b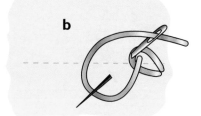

b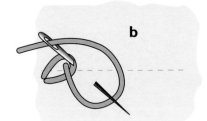

Zigzag chain stitch on a curved line

c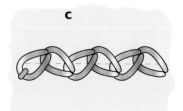

c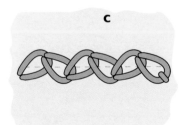

Half feather stitch

 RIGHT-HANDED

 LEFT-HANDED

• STITCHING TIP •

Be sure to take a good, sharp diagonal for your 'spikes'; if they are too upright, the stitch will look more like a lop-sided blanket stitch!

Half feather stitch on curved lines

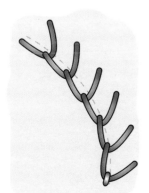

Bring the needle out on your stitching line. Insert the needle just below and to the right, and take a diagonal stitch as shown so that the needle emerges again on the stitching line, allowing the thread to loop under the needle tip (**a**).

Continue making stitches in the same way (**b**); when your stitching is complete, secure the final loop with a small straight stitch (**c**).

Bring the needle out on your stitching line. Insert the needle just below and to the left, and take a diagonal stitch as shown so that the needle emerges again on the stitching line, allowing the thread to loop under the needle tip (**a**).

Continue making stitches in the same way (**b**); when your stitching is complete, secure the final loop with a small straight stitch (**c**).

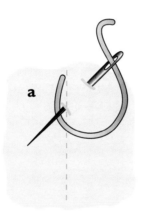

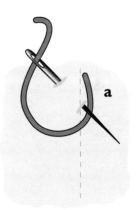

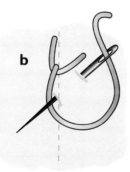

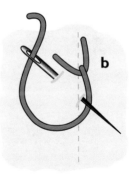

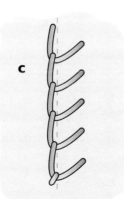

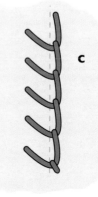

⌒ Single feather stitch ⌒

 RIGHT-HANDED

 LEFT-HANDED

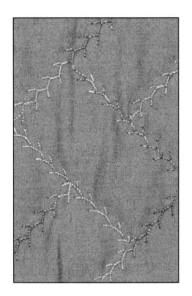

Bring the needle out slightly to the left of your stitching line. Insert the needle to the right of the stitching line, at the same level, and take a diagonal stitch as shown so that the needle emerges slightly to the right of the stitching line, allowing the thread to loop under the needle tip (**a**).

Make the second stitch in a similar way, but this time going in well to the left and emerging slightly to the left of the stitching line as shown (**b**). This ensures a staggered central line, which is prettier and more effective than a straight central line.

Continue making stitches alternately to the right and the left; when your stitching is complete, secure the final loop with a small straight stitch (**c**).

Bring the needle out slightly to the right of your stitching line. Insert the needle to the left of the stitching line, at the same level, and take a diagonal stitch as shown so that the needle emerges slightly to the left of the stitching line, allowing the thread to loop under the needle tip (**a**).

Make the second stitch in a similar way, but this time going in well to the right and emerging slightly to the right of the stitching line as shown (**b**). This ensures a staggered central line, which is prettier and more effective than a straight central line.

Continue making stitches alternately to the left and the right; when your stitching is complete, secure the final loop with a small straight stitch (**c**).

• STITCHING TIP •

The more complex feather stitches (double, triple etc) are best saved for embroidery projects rather than quilting.

⌒

a

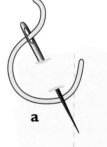
a

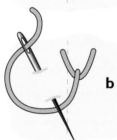
b

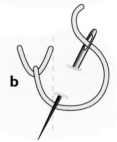
b

Single feather stitch on a curved line

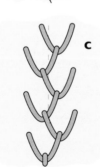
c

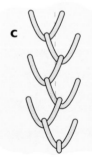
c

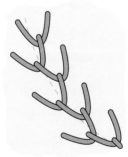

❧ *Fly stitch* ❧

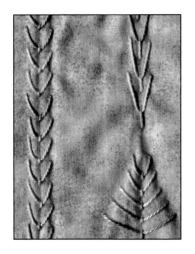

 RIGHT-HANDED

Bring the needle out to the left of the stitching line. Insert the needle an equal distance to the right of the stitching line, at the same level, so that the tip emerges on the stitching line as shown; allow the thread to loop under the needle tip (**a**).

Pull the thread through, then insert the needle further down the stitching line so that it emerges above and to the left of the stitching line as shown (**b**). Continue the same sequence along the stitching line (**c**).

 LEFT-HANDED

Bring the needle out to the right of the stitching line. Insert the needle an equal distance to the left of the stitching line, at the same level, so that the tip emerges on the stitching line as shown; allow the thread to loop under the needle tip (**a**).

Pull the thread through, then insert the needle further down the stitching line so that it emerges above and to the right of the stitching line as shown (**b**). Continue the same sequence along the stitching line (**c**).

• STITCHING TIP •

Have fun with shortening and elongating fly stitch; try making the central securing stitch so small that it's virtually invisible, or larger to become a feature.

~

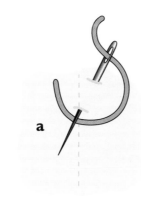

a

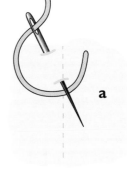

a

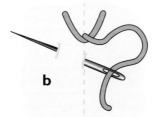

b

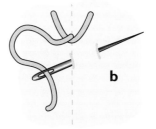

b

Fly stitch on a curved line

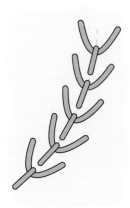

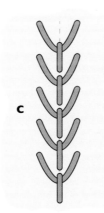

c

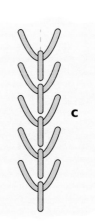

c

43

Fern stitch

RIGHT-HANDED

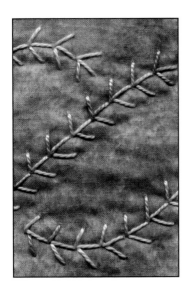

Fern stitch is formed by repeating a sequence of three straight stitches, worked in a fan shape. Bring the thread out on the stitching line, then insert the needle above and to the right to make the first stitch; insert the needle diagonally so that the tip emerges on the stitching line as shown (**a**).

Pull the thread through, then take a straight stitch down the stitching line so that it joins the start of the first stitch; insert the needle diagonally so that the tip emerges above and to the left as shown (**b**).

Insert the needle at the junction of the first two stitches to complete the first fan shape (**c**), bringing it out further along the stitching line, ready to begin the next fan (**d**). The final stitching line consists of a series of these fan shapes (**e**); make sure that each fan shape is touching the next.

The three spikes of the fan can be worked so that the diagonal stitches are slightly shorter than the central one, as shown in the sequence, or so that they are level at the top, as shown as in **f**.

• STITCHING TIP •

Note the skip from the first outward stitch across to the centre stitch. Don't be tempted to stitch each of the three parts individually; you'll use up more thread and more time, and the back of your work won't look so neat.

Fern stitch on a curved line

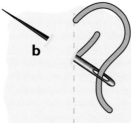
a

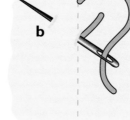
b

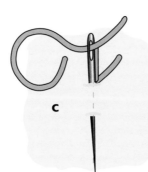
c

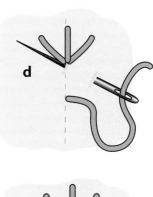
d

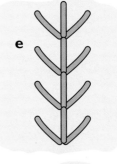
e

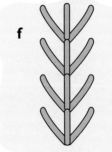
f

Fern stitch

 LEFT-HANDED

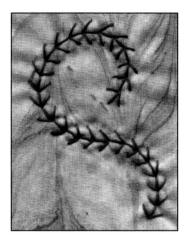

Fern stitch is formed by repeating a sequence of three straight stitches, worked in a fan shape. Bring the thread out on the stitching line, then insert the needle above and to the left to make the first stitch; insert the needle diagonally so that the tip emerges on the stitching line as shown (**a**).

Pull the thread through, then take a straight stitch down the stitching line so that it joins the start of the first stitch; insert the needle diagonally so that the tip emerges above and to the right as shown (**b**).

Insert the needle at the junction of the first two stitches to complete the first fan shape (**c**), bringing it out further along the stitching line, ready to begin the next fan (**d**). The final stitching line consists of a series of these fan shapes (**e**); make sure that each fan shape is touching the next.

The three spikes of the fan can be worked so that the diagonal stitches are slightly shorter than the central one, as shown in the sequence, or so that they are level at the top, as shown as in **f**.

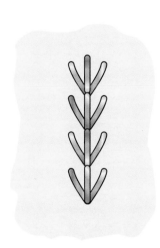

As a variation, try working your fern stitch as a narrower line with more upright 'spikes' for the diagonal stitches.

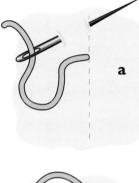
a

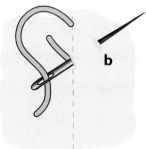
b

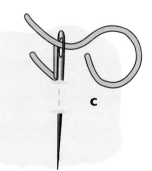
c

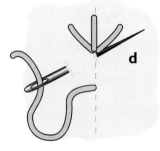
d

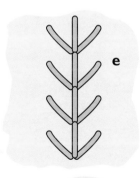
e

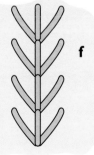
f

❧ *Blanket stitch* ❧

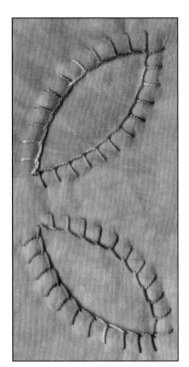

 RIGHT-HANDED

Hold your work so that the stitching line is vertical, and bring the thread out on the stitching line. Insert the needle horizontally from right to left, so that the tip emerges a short way down the stitching line as shown, allowing the thread to form a loop around the needle tip (**a**).

Pull the thread through, then continue making evenly-spaced stitches in the same way (**b**); when your stitching is complete, secure the last loop with a small straight stitch (**c**).

 LEFT-HANDED

Hold your work so that the stitching line is vertical, and bring the thread out on the stitching line. Insert the needle horizontally from left to right, so that the tip emerges a short way down the stitching line as shown, allowing the thread to form a loop around the needle tip (**a**).

Pull the thread through, then continue making evenly-spaced stitches in the same way (**b**); when your stitching is complete, secure the last loop with a small straight stitch (**c**).

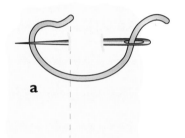

a

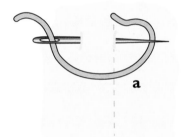

a

> **• STITCHING TIP •**
>
> *It's quicker to stitch into a loop of thread than to wrap the thread around your needle each time you take a stitch.*
>
> ❧

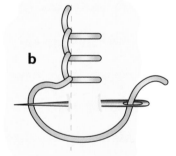

b

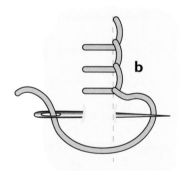

b

Blanket stitch on a curved line

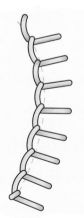

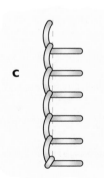

c

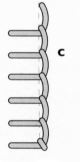

c

Blanket stitch

Blanket stitch variations

Blanket stitch is a very adaptable technique; vary it by working the stitches in pairs, or clusters of three or four, as shown in the first three examples below. You can work the clusters of stitches quite close to each other, so that they are more like buttonhole stitches.

To create a stitch that looks like a shell edging, work the stitches so that they gradually get longer and then shorter again. With a bit of practice, you'll soon get used to the rhythm of lengthening and shortening your stitches in even increments to create an evenly undulating line.

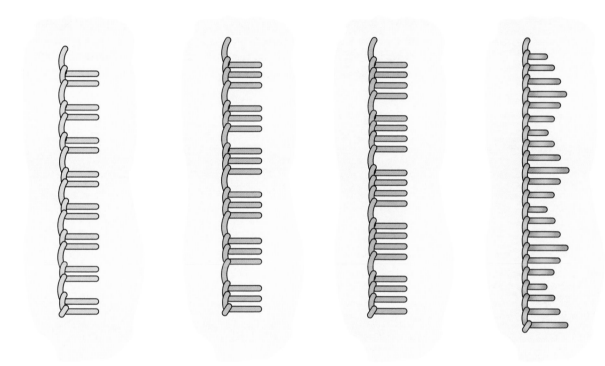

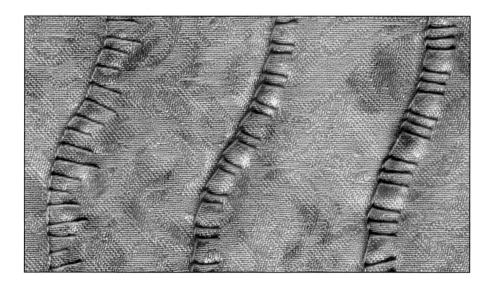

～ *Closed blanket stitch* ～

RIGHT-HANDED

Closed blanket stitch is worked in a similar way to ordinary blanket stitch, but the stitches are worked at alternating angles so that the finished effect is a series of triangular points.

Hold your work so that the stitching line is vertical, and bring the thread out on the stitching line. Insert the needle diagonally upwards from right to left as shown, so that the tip emerges a very short way down the stitching line, allowing the thread to form a loop around the needle tip (**a**).

Pull the thread through, then insert the needle at the top of the previous slanting stitch, this time so that it points diagonally downwards as shown (**b**); again, make a loop around the tip of the needle.

Pull the thread through to complete this part of the stitch, then continue alternating the slant of the stitches to create a sequence of even points (**c** and **d**); when your stitching is complete, secure the last loop with a tiny straight stitch (**e**).

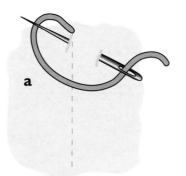

a

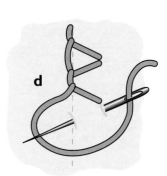

d

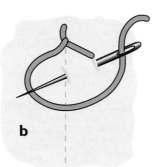

b

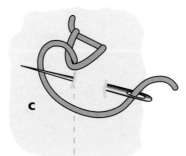

e

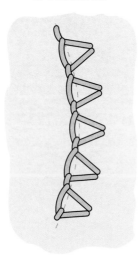

Closed blanket stitch on a curved line

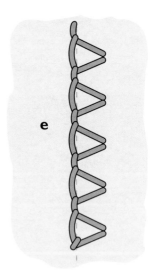

c

Closed blanket stitch

LEFT-HANDED

Closed blanket stitch is worked in a similar way to ordinary blanket stitch, but the stitches are worked at alternating angles so that the finished effect is a series of triangular points.

Hold your work so that the stitching line is vertical, and bring the thread out on the stitching line. Insert the needle diagonally upwards from left to right as shown, so that the tip emerges a very short way down the stitching line, allowing the thread to form a loop around the needle tip (**a**).

Pull the thread through, then insert the needle at the top of the previous slanting stitch, this time so that it points diagonally downwards as shown (**b**); again, make a loop around the tip of the needle.

Pull the thread through to complete this part of the stitch, then continue alternating the slant of the stitches to create a sequence of even points (**c** and **d**); when your stitching is complete, secure the last loop with a tiny straight stitch (**e**).

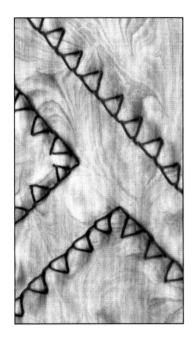

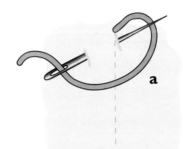

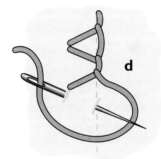

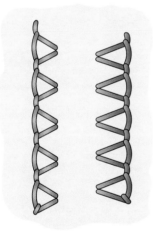

You can vary the appearance of your closed blanket stitch lines by altering the width and the interval of your triangular shapes.

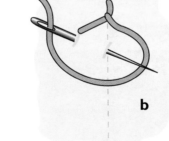

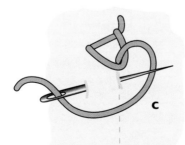

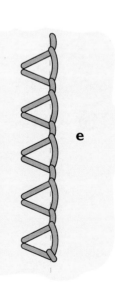

～ *Herringbone stitch* ～

 RIGHT-HANDED

Hold your work with the stitching line horizontal, and bring the thread out at the left-hand end, below the stitching line. A short distance to the right, insert the needle horizontally, right to left, above the stitching line as shown (**a**).

Now take a horizontal stitch below the stitching line and to the right (**b**). Continue working in the same way to create a line of overlapping stitches (**c**).

 LEFT-HANDED

Hold your work with the stitching line horizontal, and bring the thread out at the right-hand end, below the stitching line. A short distance to the left, insert the needle horizontally, left to right, above the stitching line as shown (**a**).

Now take a horizontal stitch below the stitching line and to the left (**b**). Continue working in the same way to create a line of overlapping stitches (**c**).

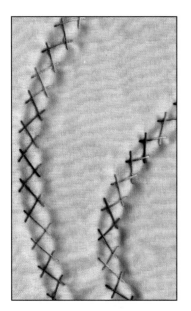

 • STITCHING TIP •

Although you're working along your stitching line in one direction, you'll see that the individual horizontal stitches are worked in the opposite direction.

～

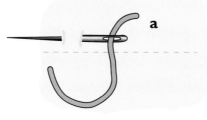

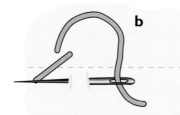

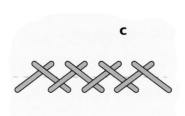

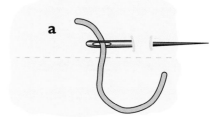

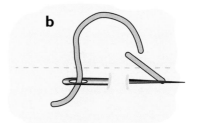

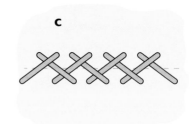

Herringbone stitch on a curved line

Herringbone stitch

 RIGHT-HANDED   **LEFT-HANDED**

Turning corners

Here's an easy way of turning a sharp corner neatly with herringbone stitch. Make your last stitch *under* the sewing-line, and follow this with a stitch *above* the line (**a**).

Turn your work (ie turn the corner), and start on this next stretch with a stitch above the line (**b**) before continuing (**c**).

To summarise: two stitches above the line will take you neatly around a corner (**d**).

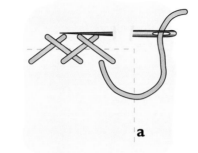
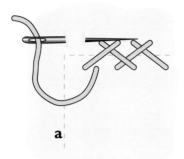
a   a

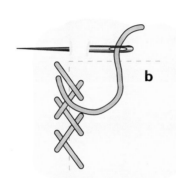
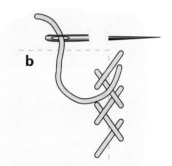
b   b

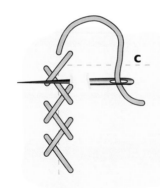
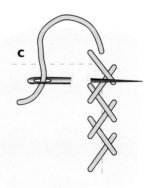
c   c

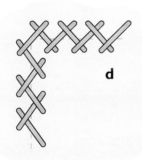
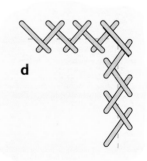
d   d

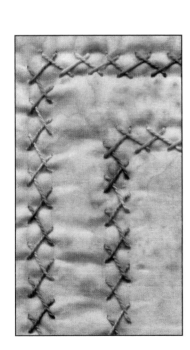

⤳ *Vandyke stitch* ⤳

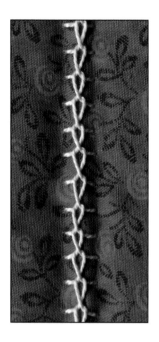

 RIGHT-HANDED

Vandyke stitch is a very effective one when you consider how easy it is to work – there are only two main stages in creating the stitch. If you find it difficult to loop through the previous stitch without catching the fabric or fibres from the thread, turn your needle round and carefully thread it through eye-first.

Hold your work with your stitching line vertical, and bring the thread out to the left of the stitching line and a short distance below the top. Take a small horizontal 'starter' stitch (**a**) across the top of the stitching line (this is the only time that this small stitch is taken).

Pull the thread through to create a long diagonal stitch on the surface. Insert the needle down the stitching line and to the right, so that the tip emerges below the first stitch as shown (**b**).

You will now be working a series of looped stitches. Take your needle over to the right-hand side and thread it behind the crossed stitches (not stitching into the fabric) (**c**), pull the thread through, and take the needle across the stitching line and down into the fabric again on the right (**d**).

Thread the needle through the previous stitch to make the next loop (**e**), and carry on in the same way to create a series of interlocking loops along your stitching line (**f**).

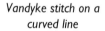
Vandyke stitch on a curved line

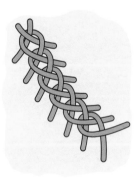

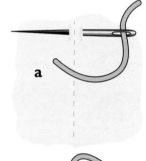

a

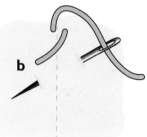

b

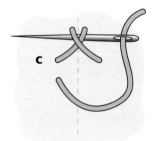

c

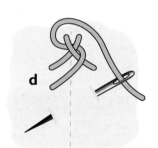

d

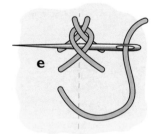

e

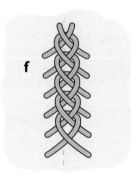

f

Vandyke stitch

LEFT-HANDED

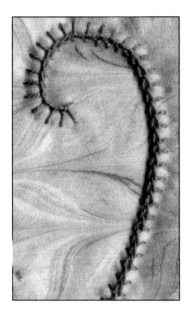

Vandyke stitch is a very effective stitch when you consider how easy it is to work – there are only two main stages in creating the stitch. If you find it difficult to loop through the previous stitch without catching the fabric or fibres from the thread, turn your needle round and carefully thread it through eye-first

Hold your work with your stitching line vertical, and bring the thread out to the right of the stitching line and a short distance below the top. Take a small horizontal 'starter' stitch (**a**) across the top of the stitching line (this is the only time that this small stitch is taken).

Pull the thread through to create a long diagonal stitch on the surface. Insert the needle down the stitching line and to the left, so that the tip emerges below the first stitch as shown (**b**).

You will now be working a series of looped stitches. Take your needle over to the left-hand side and thread it behind the crossed stitches (not stitching into the fabric) (**c**), pull the thread through, and take the needle across the stitching line and down into the fabric again on the left (**d**).

Thread the needle through the previous stitch to make the next loop (**e**), and carry on in the same way to create a series of interlocking loops along your stitching line (**f**).

• **STITCHING TIP** •

If you take your diagonal stitch too close to the central stitching line, the 'legs' that appear at the sides of the stitch will disappear, and the line of stitching will look similar to chain stitch. However, you can make a feature of these legs by widening the diagonal stitch – this looks particularly effective when you're stitching round a curve, as in the example above. Here, the diagonal stitches in the centre of the curve are more or less obscured but those outside the curve are exaggerated.

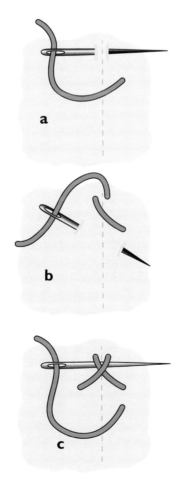

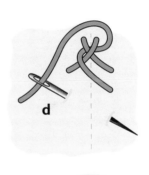

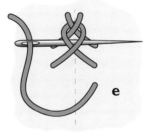

Wheatear stitch

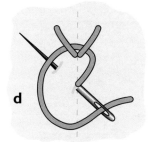 **RIGHT-HANDED**

Work with your stitching line vertical, and bring the thread out so that it emerges to the left of the line at the top. Insert the needle a little way down the centre line, and take a diagonal stitch upwards from left to right, so that the needle tip emerges an equal distance to the right (**a**).

Take a diagonal stitch back to the centre, inserting the needle vertically to emerge further down the centre line (**b**).

Pull the thread through; you now have a pair of diagonal stitches in a V shape. Make a loop by threading the needle behind this V shape from right to left (without going through the fabric) (**c**).

Pull the thread through gently and insert the needle in the centre again to complete the loop; take a diagonal stitch upwards into the fabric as shown (**d**), ready to begin working the next diagonal stitch.

Continue working the same sequence all the way down the stitching line (**e**). To finish, make a pair of diagonal stitches, then thread the V shape with a final loop.

> **• STITCHING TIP •**
>
> *When you're passing the needle behind the 'legs' of the previous stitch, note that the needle passes in front of the chain section in the centre.*

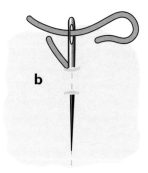

a

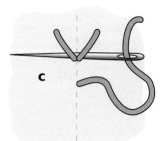

b

c

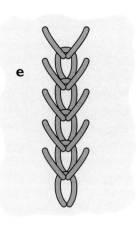

d

e

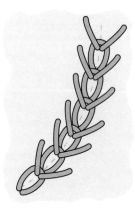

Wheatear stitch on a curved line

~ *Wheatear stitch* ~

LEFT-HANDED

Work with your stitching line vertical, and bring the thread out so that it emerges to the right of the line at the top. Insert the needle a little way down the centre line, and take a diagonal stitch upwards from right to left, so that the needle tip emerges an equal distance to the left (**a**).

Take a diagonal stitch back to the centre, inserting the needle vertically to emerge further down the centre line (**b**).

Pull the thread through; you now have a pair of diagonal stitches in a V shape. Make a loop by threading the needle behind this V shape from left to right (without going through the fabric) (**c**).

Pull the thread through gently and insert the needle in the centre again to complete the loop; take a diagonal stitch upwards into the fabric as shown (**d**), ready to begin working the next diagonal stitch.

Continue working the same sequence all the way down the stitching line (**e**). To finish, make a pair of diagonal stitches, then thread the V shape with a final loop.

• STITCHING TIP •

Wheatear stitch is a combined stitch – it's formed by making one sequence of stitches and then threading the needle through to create a loop as the final part of the stitch. In the same way as when working Vandyke stitch, you might find it easier when you're creating the loops to turn the needle round and thread it through the previous stitches eye-first.

a

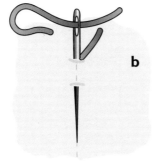

b

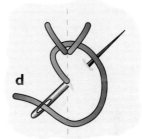

d

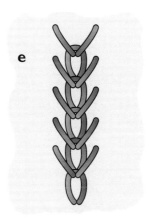

e

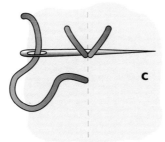

c

⌒ Long-armed cross stitch ⌒

 RIGHT-HANDED

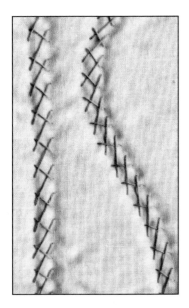

Work with your stitching line vertical, and bring the thread out so that it emerges a short way to the left of the stitching line. Take a long diagonal stitch across and down the line, inserting the needle horizontally to straddle the stitching line as shown (**a**).

Half-way up the first long diagonal stitch, insert the needle horizontally again (**b**); this will create a shorter diagonal stitch in the opposite direction when you pull it through.

Take another long stitch down the centre line (**c**); this will cross the previous short stitch. Continue the same sequence, taking long diagonal stitches downwards and shorter ones upwards (**d**), to create a line of meshed stitches (**e**).

> **• STITCHING TIP •**
>
> *You must be brave enough to take a long stitch at stage **a**, so that the second stitch, taken at stage **b**, can cut across it half-way. If you don't the stitch will look more like conventional cross stitch.*
>
> ⌒

a

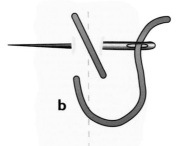

b

c

d

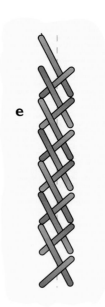

e

Long-armed cross stitch

 LEFT-HANDED

Work with your stitching line vertical, and bring the thread out so that it emerges a short way to the right of the stitching line. Take a long diagonal stitch across and down the line, inserting the needle horizontally to straddle the stitching line as shown (**a**).

Half-way up the first long diagonal stitch, insert the needle horizontally again (**b**); this will create a shorter diagonal stitch in the opposite direction when you pull it through.

Take another long stitch down the centre line (**c**); this will cross the previous short stitch. Continue the same sequence, taking long diagonal stitches downwards and shorter ones upwards (**d**), to create a line of meshed stitches (**e**).

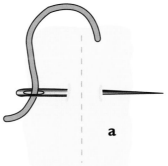

a

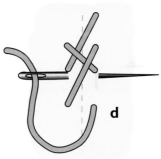

d

Long-armed cross stitch on a curved line

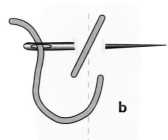

b

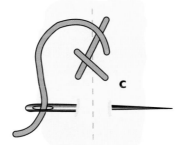

c

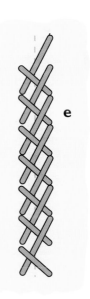

e

❦ *Open Cretan stitch* ❦

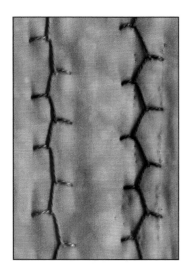

 RIGHT-HANDED

Work with your stitching line horizontal, and bring the thread out at the end. Move the needle along the central line, and take a short vertical stitch upwards (**a**), letting the thread loop round the tip of the needle.

Move the needle along the stitching line, and take a short vertical stitch downwards (**b**), again allowing the thread to loop round the needle tip.

Now take another stitch on the other side of the line (**c**), and continue in the same way, alternating looped stitches to the top and bottom of the central line (**d**).

 LEFT-HANDED

Work with your stitching line horizontal, and bring the thread out at the end. Move the needle along the central line, and take a short vertical stitch upwards (**a**), letting the thread loop round the tip of the needle.

Move the needle along the stitching line, and take a short vertical stitch downwards (**b**), again allowing the thread to loop round the needle tip.

Now take another stitch on the other side of the line (**c**), and continue in the same way, alternating looped stitches to the top and bottom of the central line (**d**).).

• STITCHING TIP •

Don't be tempted to work this stitch too widely on quilt projects, otherwise the threads will become loose and may snag.

Open Cretan stitch is also a very effective stitch for joining the different panels of wall-hangings; it creates an open mesh (see the photograph on page 17).

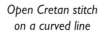

Open Cretan stitch on a curved line

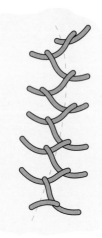

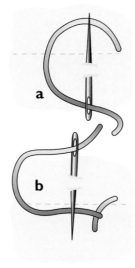

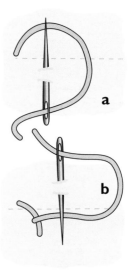

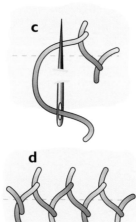

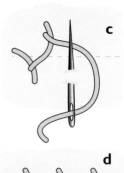

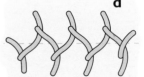

❧ *Coral stitch* ❧

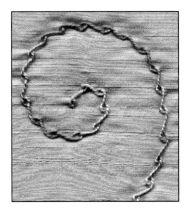

 RIGHT-HANDED

Working from right to left, bring the needle out at the right-hand end of your stitching line. Move the needle along the stitching line to the left and take a small diagonal stitch, looping the thread over and then under the needle as shown (**a**).

Gently pull the knot tight, then take another stitch in the same way at an equal distance along the line (**b**).

Continue in the same way, creating knotted stitches at regular intervals (**c**). Finish the stitching line with a long stitch after the final knot.

 LEFT-HANDED

Working from left to right, bring the needle out at the left-hand end of your stitching line. Move the needle along the stitching line to the right and take a small diagonal stitch, looping the thread over and then under the needle as shown (**a**).

Gently pull the knot tight, then take another stitch in the same way at an equal distance along the line (**b**).

Continue in the same way, creating knotted stitches at regular intervals (**c**). Finish the stitching line with a long stitch after the final knot.

• STITCHING TIP •

It's quite tricky to keep coral stitch even if you take a sharp diagonal for your stitch; just take a shallow diagonal each time, and the knots on the final stitching line will look better.

❧

Coral stitch on a curved line

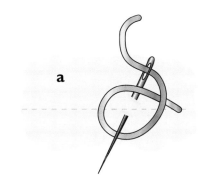

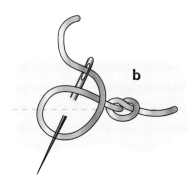

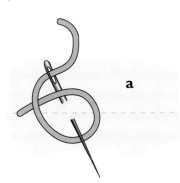

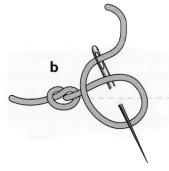

⮜ *Sword-edged stitch* ⮞

 RIGHT-HANDED

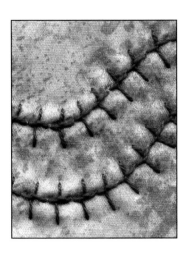

Work this stitch horizontally along your stitching line. Bring the needle out on the stitching line, then insert it below and to the left, taking a diagonal stitch back to the central line as shown (**a**). Leave the stitch slightly slack.

Take the thread across the diagonal stitch and loop the needle and thread under the stitch from the right to the left as shown (**b**). Take the needle into the work above the stitching line (**c**).

Pull the needle through to finish the first stitch; you now have an elongated crossed stitch (**d**); the four points of the stitch create a long diamond shape. Continue in the same way (**e**), making pairs of loops along the stitching line (**f**).

Sword-edged stitch on a curved line

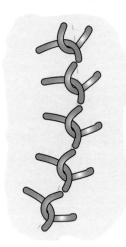

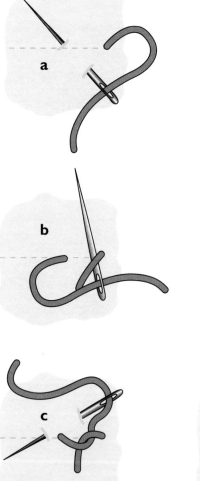

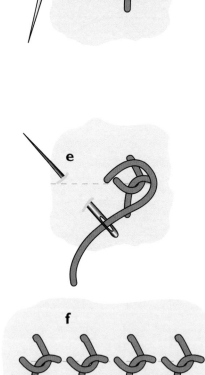

⌣ *Sword-edged stitch* ⌣

 LEFT-HANDED

Work this stitch horizontally along your stitching line. Bring the needle out on the stitching line, then insert it below and to the right, taking a diagonal stitch back to the central line as shown (**a**). Leave the stitch slightly slack.

Take the thread across the diagonal stitch and loop the needle and thread under the stitch from the left to the right as shown (**b**). Take the needle into the work above the stitching line (**c**).

Pull the needle through to finish the first stitch; you now have an elongated crossed stitch (**d**); the four points of the stitch create a long diamond shape. Continue in the same way (**e**), making pairs of loops along the stitching line (**f**).

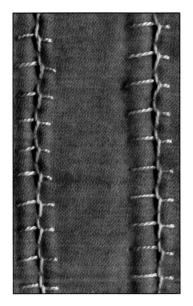

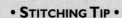

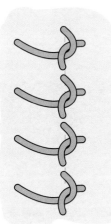

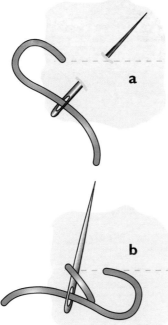

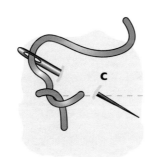

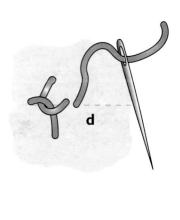

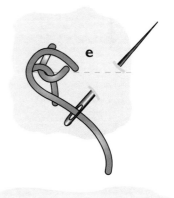

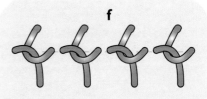

~ Chevron stitch ~

 RIGHT-HANDED

Working from the left-hand end of your stitching line, bring the needle out below the stitching line. Move the needle along to the right, and insert it from right to left above the stitching line (**a**). This creates a long diagonal stitch.

Insert the needle again horizontally from right to left so that the needle tip emerges at the top of the

diagonal stitch (**b**); keep the needle tip underneath the loop of thread.

Take the needle to the right and below the stitching line; as before, make two short horizontal stitches from right to left (**c** and **d**). Continue in the same way along the stitching line (**e**) to create a chevron pattern (**f**).

> **• STITCHING TIP •**
>
> *Chevron stitch isn't suitable for very strong curves, as it's hard to keep the stitch pattern consistent, but it works well on gentle curves.*
>
> ~

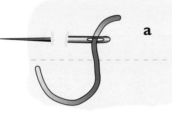

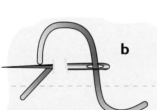

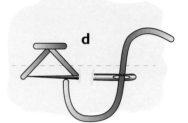

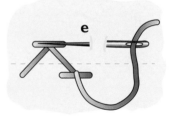

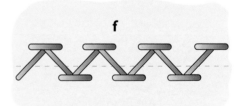

Chevron stitch on a curved line

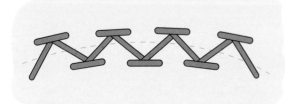

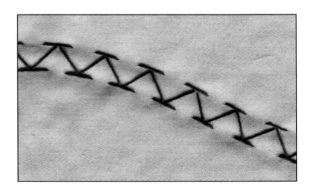

~ *Chevron stitch* ~

LEFT-HANDED

• STITCHING TIP •

If you work very long straight stitches at the top and bottom of the stitching, you create a more solid line of stitching; or, if you prefer, you can make the straight stitches very short.

Working from the right-hand end of your stitching line, bring the needle out below the stitching line. Move the needle along to the left, and insert it from left to right above the stitching line (**a**). This creates a long diagonal stitch.

Insert the needle again horizontally from left to right so that the needle tip emerges at the top of the diagonal stitch (**b**); keep the needle tip underneath the loop of thread.

Take the needle to the left and below the stitching line; as before, make two short horizontal stitches from left to right (**c** and **d**). Continue in the same way along the stitching line (**e**) to create a chevron pattern (**f**).

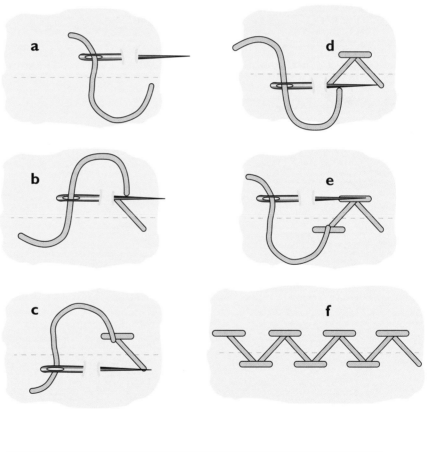

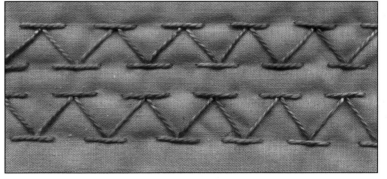

~ *Double knot stitch* ~

 RIGHT-HANDED

Working with your stitching line horizontal, bring the thread out at the right-hand end of your stitching line. Take the needle further along the stitching line and take a small vertical stitch downwards (**a**).

Pull the stitch through, then take the needle and thread under this first stitch from top to bottom (**b**). Pull

that loop through gently, then take the needle under the first stitch and over the loop as shown, again working from top to bottom (**c**).

Pull this second loop through, and continue working along your stitching line in the same way (**d** and **e**); this creates a line of stitching with knots at even intervals (**f**).

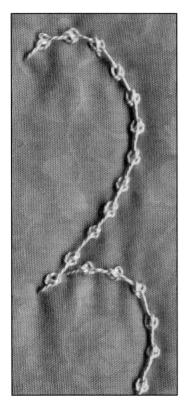

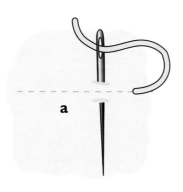

a

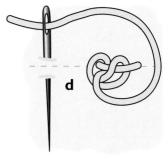

d

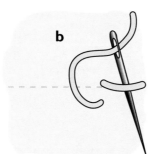

b

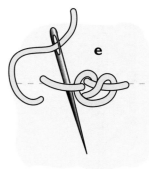

e

c

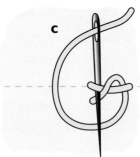

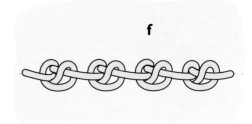

f

Double knot stitch

 LEFT-HANDED

Working with your stitching line horizontal, bring the thread out at the left-hand end of your stitching line. Take the needle further along the stitching line and take a small vertical stitch downwards (**a**).

Pull the stitch through, then take the needle and thread under this first stitch from top to bottom (**b**). Pull

that loop through gently, then take the needle under the first stitch and over the loop as shown, again working from top to bottom (**c**).

Pull this second loop through, and continue working along your stitching line in the same way (**d** and **e**); this creates a line of stitching with knots at even intervals (**f**).

• STITCHING TIP •

If you pull your thread through gently in the direction of your stitching, this will help your double knots lie neatly along the stitching line. If they fall to one side, it's easy to push them back in line with your fingernail.

Double knot stitch on a curved line

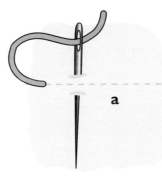

a

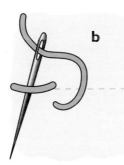

b

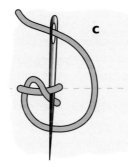

c

d

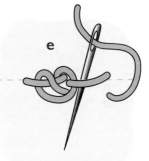

e

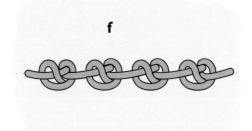

f

Extra techniques

As well as the stitches shown in the previous section, you can also try out these extra stitches and techniques; use them alongside the QWAD stitches to create visual interest or as fillings.

Couching

Couching is suitable for threads that won't easily pass through the three layers of your quilt; couching stitches can be simple single stitches or worked in clusters. If you're couching very wide threads, or multiple threads together, try catching them down with decorative stitches such as fern or fly stitch.

Filling stitches

One particular advantage of filling stitches is that they can fill in any size or shape of stitching area; it doesn't have to be a regular shape. Seeding stitches can be made almost any size, from quite small, barely-there little dots right up to quite large stitches. Don't forget to try knots, too, for filling in empty areas of your design; both French knots and bullion knots work well and give added texture (do double-check the difference between the two – it's surprising how many people think they are sewing a French knot when they have actually been wrapping a bullion knot).

Beading

On my travels, along with collecting threads (and fabrics), I do treat myself to a little pack of beads or buttons now and again – after all, a little retail therapy goes a long way! Beautiful to look at and to collect, they can often add that extra little bit of tactile interest to a 'project in need' when used for seeding or even for a linear outline.

Shisha

Little mirrors add a wonderful flash to your work, and combine very well with Quilting With A Difference; in this section you'll find three different ways of attaching the shisha.

∿ Couching ∾

 RIGHT-HANDED **LEFT-HANDED**

Couching means catching a thread down on the surface of your work with a series of stitches in a different thread. This technique works well for any threads which won't easily pass through three layers.

The stitches you use to secure the chunky thread can be simple, single stitches (**a**), or clusters of stitches (**b**), and you can couch in straight lines, curves (**c**) or spirals (**d**). If the thread to be couched is particularly wide or made up of multiple fibres, you could use a decorative embroidery stitch such as fly stitch (see page 43), as shown in **e**, or fern stitch (see pages 44-45),

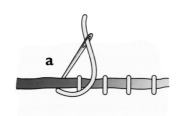 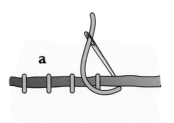

 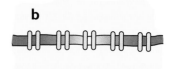

 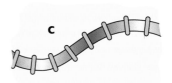

• STITCHING TIP •

If your aim is to quilt as well as to decorate while you're couching, remember that your couching stitch will need to pass through all three layers of your quilt sandwich.

∽

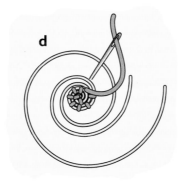 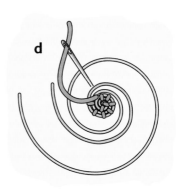

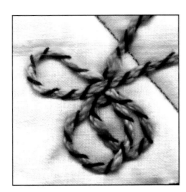 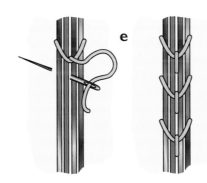 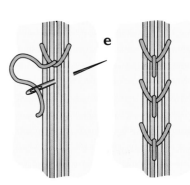

❦ Seeding ❧

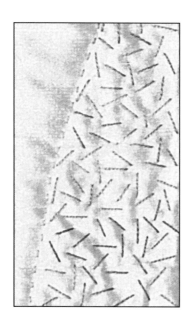

 RIGHT-HANDED

Bring the thread out to the surface of the fabric, somewhere near the right-hand edge of the area to be filled. Take a straight stitch of your chosen length across the surface of the fabric; bring the needle up a short distance away from the first stitch, in any direction (**a**).

Take another stitch, the same length as the first one but at a different angle (**b**). Continue making straight stitches at varying angles in the same way, until the stitching area is covered (**c**).

 LEFT-HANDED

Bring the thread out to the surface of the fabric, somewhere near the left-hand edge of the area to be filled. Take a straight stitch of your chosen length across the surface of the fabric; bring the needle up a short distance away from the first stitch, in any direction (**a**).

Take another stitch, the same length as the first one but at a different angle (**b**). Continue making straight stitches at varying angles in the same way, until the stitching area is covered (**c**).

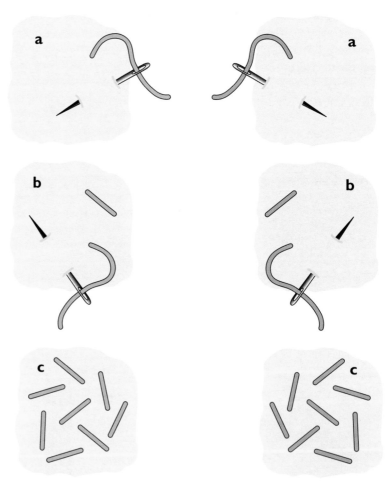

Seeding variations

Seeding stitches can add textural quilting – try tiny, dot-like seeding as well as larger stitches. I tend to use a maximum length of half an inch or one centimetre for quilt projects.

∽ Seeding ∾

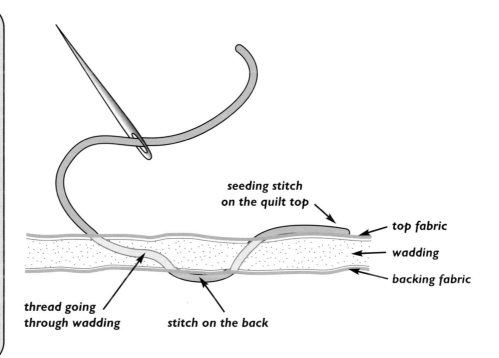

• STITCHING TIP •

If you are using your seeding to quilt as well as to decorate, take a stitch through all three layers to secure them at some point after each surface seeding stitch. If necessary, this quilting stitch can be a small, neat stitch through the layers, followed by meandering your needle through the wadding to the next area to be stitched, as shown.

This technique also applies to seeding with knots and beading.

seeding stitch on the quilt top

top fabric

wadding

backing fabric

thread going through wadding

stitch on the back

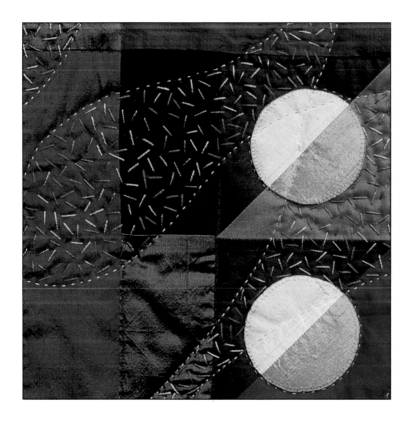

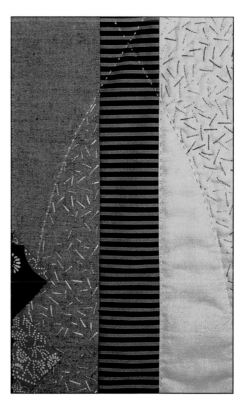

~ French knots ~

 RIGHT-HANDED   **LEFT-HANDED**

Bring the needle to the front of the fabric, then wrap the thread around the tip of the needle two or three times (**a**). Pull the needle through the twists of thread (**b**), then take the needle down into the fabric (**c**). As you pull the needle through, the twists will form a knot on the surface of the fabric (**d**). Scatter the knots randomly across the area to be filled (**e**).

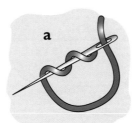
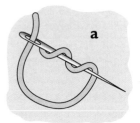

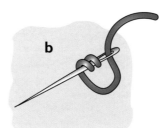
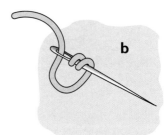

• STITCHING TIPS •

*Remember that, with French knots, the thread is wrapped around the needle **before** you take a stitch into the fabric.*

Try different thicknesses of thread and different numbers of needle 'wraps' to create them.

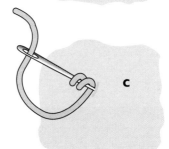

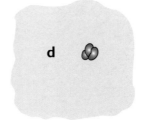
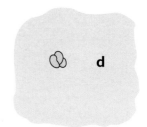

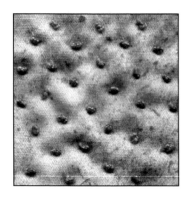

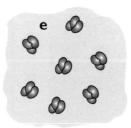
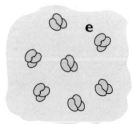

❧ *Bullion knots* ❧

Bring the needle to the front of the fabric, then insert the needle into the fabric as shown (**a**) – like taking a long backstitch. Wrap the thread around the tip of the needle several times (**b**).

Pull the needle carefully through the twists of thread (**c**) to form a long knot along the thread; then take the needle down into the fabric at the beginning of the stitch to secure the knot (**d**). The final effect is a long knot that lies flat on your work (**e**).

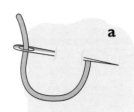

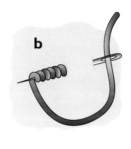
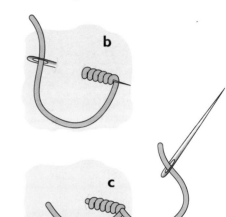

• STITCHING TIP •

Pulling the twists of thread along the stitch may seem tricky at first, but you'll soon get the hang of it; a bit of gentle help from your fingernail will make sure that the twists lie evenly along the thread.

❧

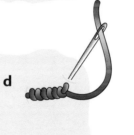
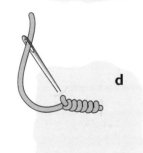

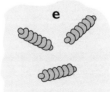

Four-legged knot stitch

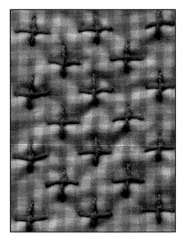

Bring the thread to the front of the work. Insert the needle directly under this point but a little way away, so that the tip emerges diagonally above and to one side as shown (**a**).

Pull the thread through to form a straight stitch. Take the needle and thread under the straight stitch, looping the thread under the needle tip as shown (**b**).

Gently pull the knot taut, then take the needle down to the side of the stitch (**c**) to complete the knot (**d**). Work the knots at regular or irregular intervals across the area to be filled (**e**).

• STITCHING TIP •

The ends of the four 'legs' that make up each knot form a diamond shape or a square shape, according to preference.

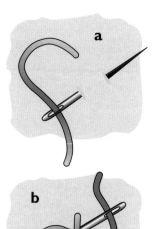
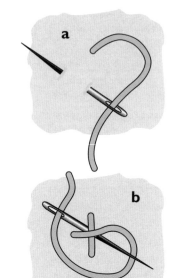

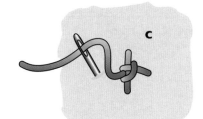
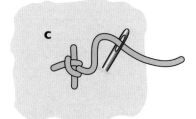

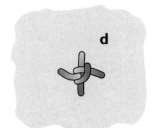
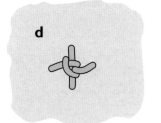

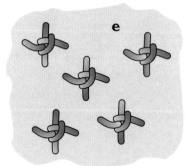
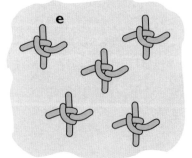

Beading

Beads can offer a more tactile alternative to using threads and knots for areas of seeding – although it may be best to save them for your more decorative work. Try collecting beads in different shapes and sizes, as well as in a variety of colours.

There are two basic ways of attaching the beads. For the first method (**a** and **b**), thread the beads onto a single thread, then catch this down with small stitches between the beads. For the second method (**c** and **d**) thread an individual bead and then take a stitch to catch it onto the fabric, looping the thread under the tip of the needle.

> **• STITCHING TIP •**
>
> *Before threading your needle ready for working with beads, make sure that the eye of your needle (the thickest part) will pass easily through the hole in the bead!*

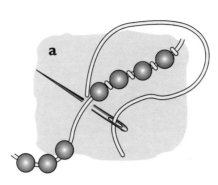

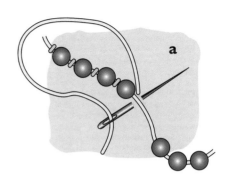

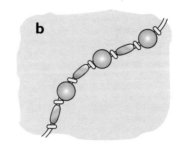

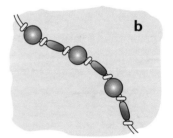

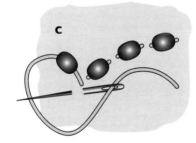

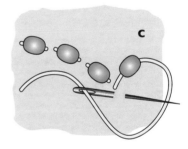

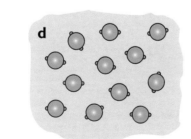

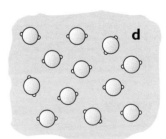

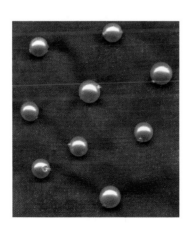

RIGHT-HANDED   **LEFT-HANDED**

Position the mirror on the fabric and work two long horizontal stitches across it. Bring the thread out at the bottom of the mirror and to one side, then loop the needle under each horizontal stitch in turn (**a**); do the same at the other side of the mirror to create a grid across the front (**b**).

Bring the needle out at the edge of the mirror. Take a stitch into the base grid (**c**), then follow this with a looped stitch into the fabric just next to the mirror's edge (**d**). Take another stitch into the grid (**e**), and continue alternating these with small looped stitches into the fabric until the mirror edge is totally enclosed (**f**).

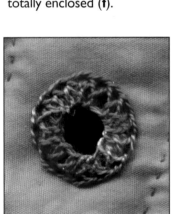

• STITCHING TIP •

For all methods of attaching shisha, make sure that you keep the grid of base stitches very tight; if it's loose, your embroidery will pull the base grid over the edge of the mirror.

a 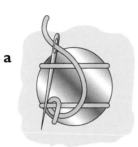   **a**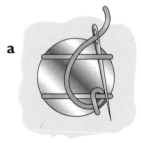

b 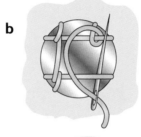   **b**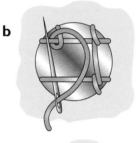

c 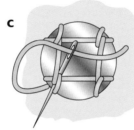   **c**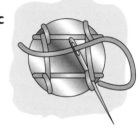

d 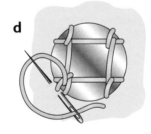   **d**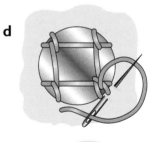

e    **e**

f 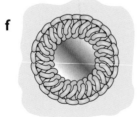   **f**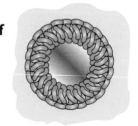

~ *Shisha 2* ~

 **RIGHT-HANDED**  **LEFT-HANDED**

Position the mirror on the fabric and work a square grid of horizontal and vertical stitches around the edges (**a**). Bring the thread out at the bottom of the mirror and to one side, then take a stitch into the grid, looping the thread under the needle tip like a blanket or buttonhole stitch (**b**).

Now take another buttonhole stitch into the fabric (**c**). As you pull the stitch through the fabric, lay the thread back and across the mirror; the stitch will then lie snugly up against the rim of the mirror.

Continue alternating stitches into the grid (**d**) and the fabric (**e**) until the mirror edge is totally enclosed (**f**).

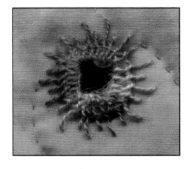

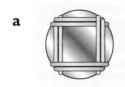 a 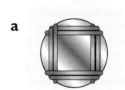 a

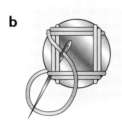 b 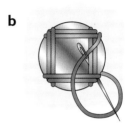 b

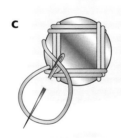 c 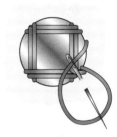 c

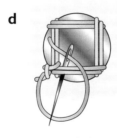 d  d

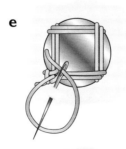 e  e

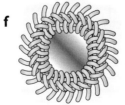 f  f

> **• STITCHING TIP •**
>
> *If you find it tricky keeping the mirror in position on your fabric while you stitch the base grid, stick a tiny piece of double-sided tape to the back of the mirror; it will hold the shisha firmly while you concentrate on your stitching.*
>
> ~

Shisha 3

 **RIGHT-HANDED**  **LEFT-HANDED**

Position the mirror on the fabric and work three vertical and three horizontal stitches across it to hold it in place (**a**). Keep this base grid of stitches nice and tight (**b**).

Beginning anywhere on the circumference, work a line of chain stitches alongside the edge of the mirror (**c** and **d**); when the circuit is complete, finish off with a tiny straight stitch to secure the final link of the chain (**e**).

> **• STITCHING TIP •**
>
> *This is a contemporary American method of shisha embroidery. As the stitching doesn't cover the edges of the mirrors, it's best to use this technique for mirrors with totally smooth edges.*

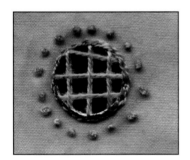

a 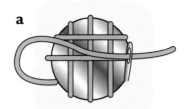   **a**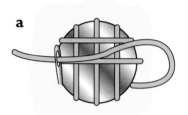

b 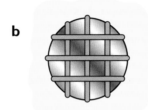   **b**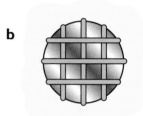

c 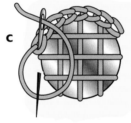   **c**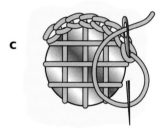

d 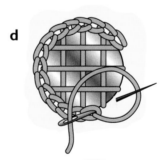   **d**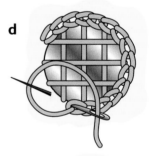

e 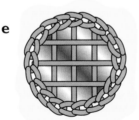   **e**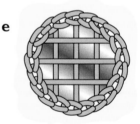

Sampler designs

Make good use of your stitching experiments!

MAKING little samples is an excellent way of trying out different Quilting With A Difference stitches and threads, but you don't want to waste all that hard work; why not build your samples into a little hanging of their own? If you'd like to use your trial blocks for a wall-hanging, try one of the layouts shown here – or copy one from the projects section (see pages 80-115). If you want to add hanging loops, see the instructions on page 138.

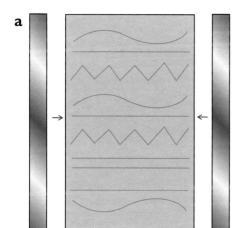

LAYOUT A

A rectangular (or square) piece of fabric can be framed by adding border strips to the sides (**a**), and then to the top and bottom (**b**).

Layer the bordered fabric with wadding and backing fabric, tack the layers (**c**), then try out your QWAD stitches. When you've finished stitching, bind the layers into a finished quilt (**d**) and remove the tacking.

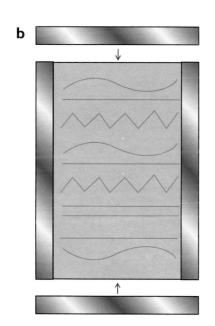

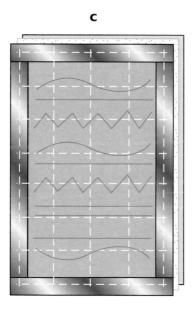

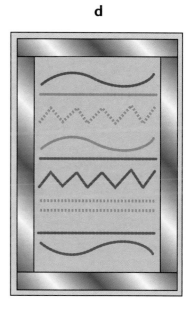

LAYOUT B

Three (or more) blocks look effective joined into a long wall-hanging. Add short strips of sashing between the blocks and at the top and bottom (**a** and **b**), then add longer strips at the sides (**c** and **d**). Layer the bordered blocks with wadding and backing fabric and tack the layers together, then work your QWAD stitches (**e**); when your stitching is complete, bind the quilt and remove the tacking (**f**).

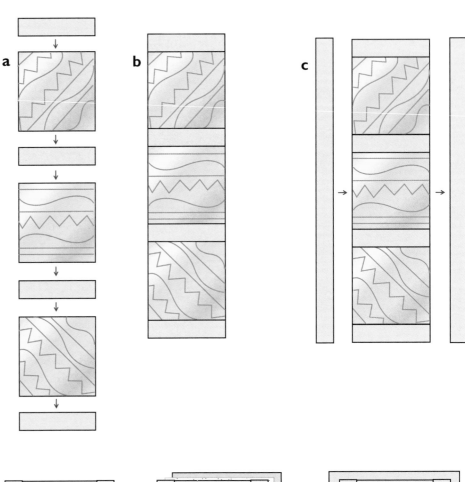

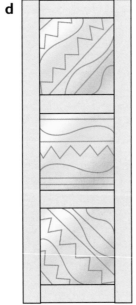

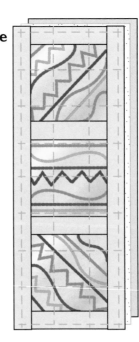

LAYOUT C

Multiple blocks can be built into quite a large quilt. Add short strips of sashing between the blocks and at the ends to create rows (**a**), then join the rows with longer strips of sashing (**b**). Mark up designs either onto the individual blocks and stitch them (**c**), or mark and stitch one large design across the front of the quilt (**d**).

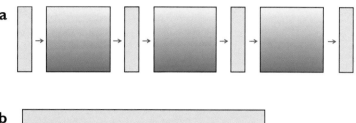

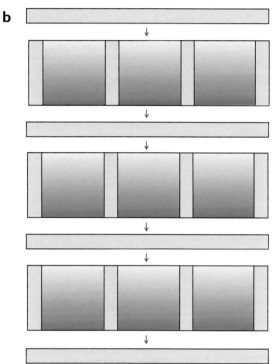

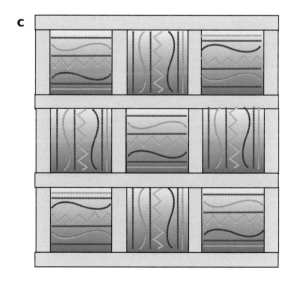

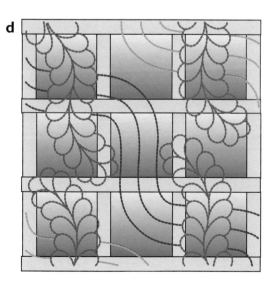

Projects

Now that you've tried out lots of Quilting With A Difference stitches, take a look at these projects. What better way to display your newly-acquired skills?

General tips for the projects

* All fabric measurements given for these projects are based on standard fabric width of 44in/112cm. If you use existing fabric from your workbox, or buy new fabric with a different width, the fabric requirements will vary – in this case, it's best to look at the measurements given under the individual project's sub-heading marked 'cutting.'

* You can use the full-size quilting designs that I've included within each project, or add your own choices

* All the project instructions are based on using seam allowances of *either* ¼in *or* 1cm. Don't be tempted to mix the imperial and metric measurements within one project: choose one measurement system and stick with it throughout.

* If you're using a quilting stencil, the design can be marked either before or after layering your fabric sandwich (you may find that the added stability created by the layering can make the process easier). If, on the other hand, you have a design on paper that needs tracing onto your fabric, you will need to do this *before* you layer your sandwich.

* If your fabric is pale enough you may be able to lay it over your design and trace through the fabric. If the fabric is dark a lightbox can be a great help. If you don't own a lightbox (and most of us don't …) the easiest alternative is to use a window in daylight. Tape your design to the glass using masking tape, then centre your fabric over the design; secure this also with masking tape, making sure that the fabric is fairly taut. You should then be able to see the design underneath and trace it through onto your fabric surface.

Quilted cards

These little card designs are an easy way to try out your Quilting With A Difference skills on a couple of small projects. Use a firm, compressed wadding so that you still create a quilted feel with your stitching but the finished fabric sandwich isn't too thick.

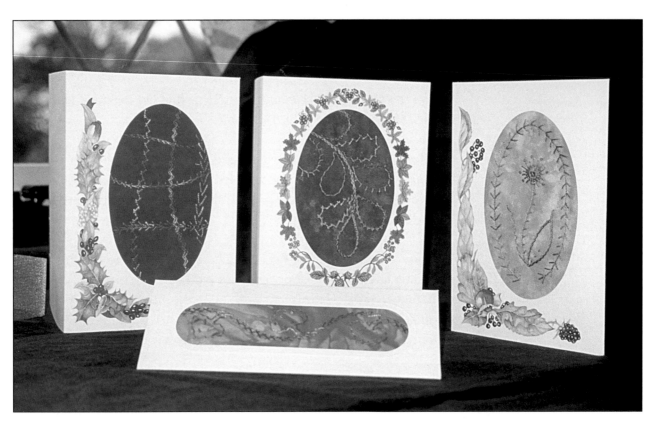

Aperture cards from
Craft Creations

✏ Fabric requirements

For each large card you will need:

- 6½ x 4½in (16 x 12cm) of background fabric
- 6½ x 4½in (16 x 12cm) of compressed wadding
- 6½ x 4½in (16 x 12cm) of butter muslin
  (for the long card, all the above should be 7 x 3in/18 x 7.5cm)

✏ Additional requirements

- Quilting thread and needle
- Quilting design (see page 85)
- Fabric marker
- Card blank with an oval aperture measuring approximately 3 x 5in (8 x 12.5cm) (or for the bookmark, 5½ x 1½in /14 x 4cm)
- Double-sided sticky tape

Instructions

1 Trace your chosen design onto the background fabric (**a**). Lay the butter muslin on a flat surface and cover it with the wadding, then lay your marked design on top; pin or tack the three layers together (**b**). Stitch the design using your choice of QWAD stitches.

2 Unfold the flaps of the card blank (**c**). Turn the card blank face down, and cut some short lengths of double-sided sticky tape; stick these around the edge of the aperture (**d**).

3 Lay your design face up on your work surface, then peel the protective papers off the pieces of double-sided tape (**e**). Hold the card mount, sticky side down, over the stitching and centre the design in the aperture; once you're satisfied with the positioning, press the card firmly in place (**f**).

4 Turn the card over so that the back of the design is towards you, and trim the edges of the three layers (fabric, wadding and muslin) to at least ½in (1cm) away from the top and bottom of the card and from the folds (**g**).

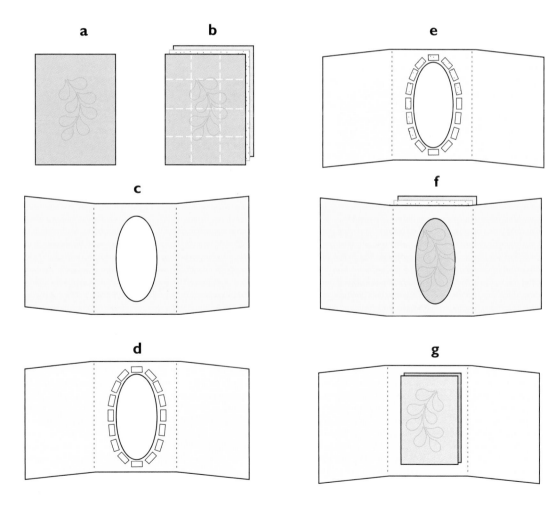

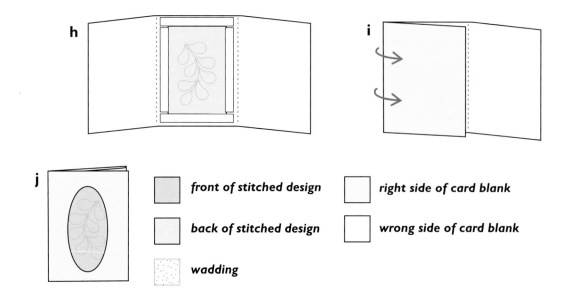

h

i

j

front of stitched design

back of stitched design

wadding

right side of card blank

wrong side of card blank

5 Add long strips of double-sided sticky tape around the edges of the central panel, covering the edges of the fabric if necessary (**h**). Peel off the backing papers, then fold the left-hand flap of the card into the centre (**i**); press it firmly onto the pieces of sticky tape to secure it. Finally, fold in the right-hand flap – this is where you can add your greetings. Your card is now finished (**j**).

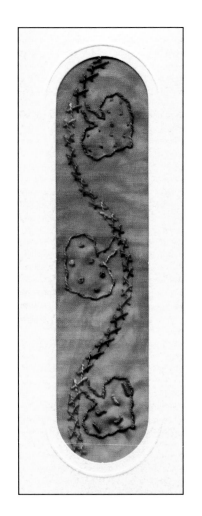

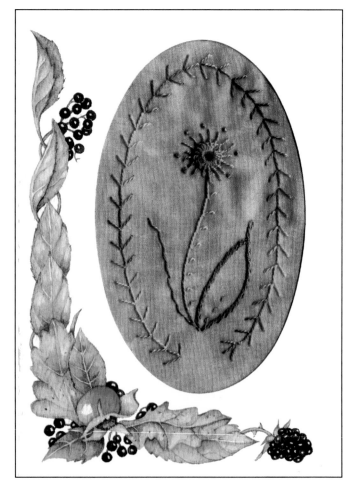

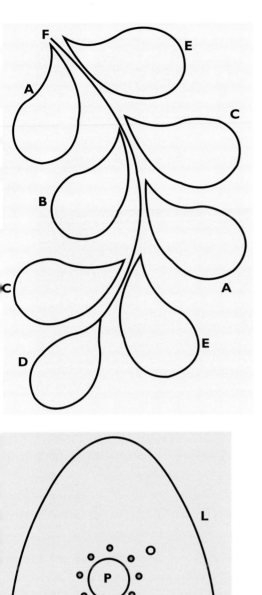

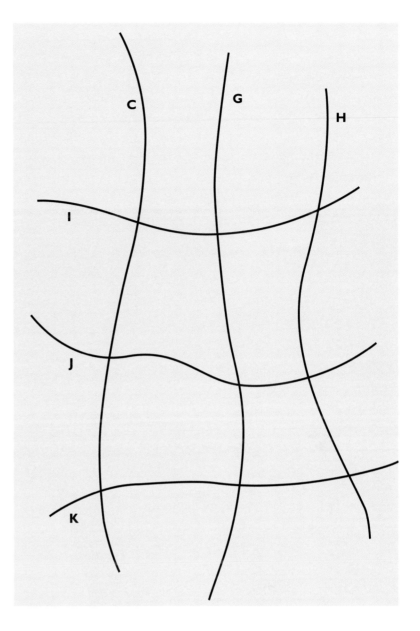

These are the stitches I used on the card designs in the photographs; you can use your own selection if you prefer.

A blanket stitch
B whipped running stitch
C herringbone stitch
D whipped chain stitch
E double knot stitch
F chain stitch
G zigzag chain stitch
H fly stitch
I chain stitch
J Vandyke stitch
K wheatear stitch
L fern stitch
M half feather stitch
N running stitch
O French knots
P shisha
Q seeding
R bullion knots

Silk cushions

*You can make these silk cushion covers as plain or as fancy as you like;
I've quilted four examples using the same design but different
stitching styles.*

Photo: Lynsey Piff

The four cushion covers in the photograph show just how much
difference you can achieve with your quilting when you vary not only
the threads but also the stitches you use. (And, of course, altering the
colour of the background fabric allows for even more variety.)

Blue silk (far right): this design creates a quiet and subtle effect.
Traditional hand-quilting using space-dyed threads.

Purple silk (second from left): a little stronger. Quilted as before, but I've
given the stitches more emphasis by threading back along sections of
them with the same thread.

Gold silk (second from right): the full Monty. The whole design has
been stitched using Quilting With A Difference alternative stitching.

Lilac silk (far left): the full Monty and more! QWAD stitching with
further surface embellishment using shisha (mirror) work.

Finished dimensions: 18in (45cm) square

> Whenever you need a 20in (50cm) square of fabric, a fat quarter-metre of standard-width fabric will give you just enough. A fat quarter-yard, on the other hand, is slightly too small, as it will be only 22 × 18in (56 × 46cm).

✏ **Fabric requirements**

For each cushion you will need:

- 20in (50cm) square of dress-weight dupion silk in your chosen colour
- 20in (50cm) square of butter muslin
- 20in (50cm) square of wadding (suitable for hand-quilting)
- 20in (50cm) of fabric for the cushion backing (calico, or other fabric of your choice)
- 10in (long quarter-metre) of toning fabric for the binding

✏ **Additional requirements**

- Quilting design: you can either use the pattern shown (see diagram on page 88), or one of your own design measuring roughly 12-15in (30-38cm) square
- Fabric-marking tool
- Quilting thread and needle
- Cushion pad measuring 18in (45cm) square

Instructions

1 Press the dupion silk carefully, then using your fabric marking pen/pencil, draw your quilting design onto the silk as shown in diagram **a** below (see the notes on transferring designs on pages 19-21).

2 Following the instructions on page 128, tack your project layers together (**b**) and quilt your design, either traditionally or with QWAD alternative quilting stitches. I've included on page 89 a plan of the stitches that I used in my busier cushion, the gold one – you may decide to follow this, or alter the stitch selection to suit your own taste. (Don't forget that you can use seeding and beading to fill in open areas if you wish.)

a

b

c

3 When you're happy that you have quilted your cushion panel enough, turn to page 132 and follow the instructions for quick and easy cushion construction. Once your cushion cover has the binding attached and finished (**c**), you can remove your tacking threads, insert the cushion pad and display your work.

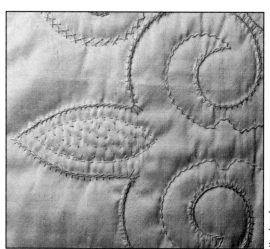

Photo: Lynsey Piff

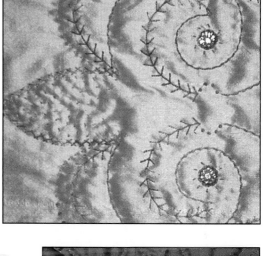

The pattern opposite is a quarter of the whole design; trace four repeats of the pattern onto your fabric, so that the repeats meet along the dotted lines as shown above.

These are the stitches I used on the gold cushion; try this arrangement, or design your own. The asterisk indicates where I've changed from one stitch to another.

A herringbone stitch **B** chain stitch **C** Vandyke stitch
D whipped running stitch **E** running stitch **F** seeding

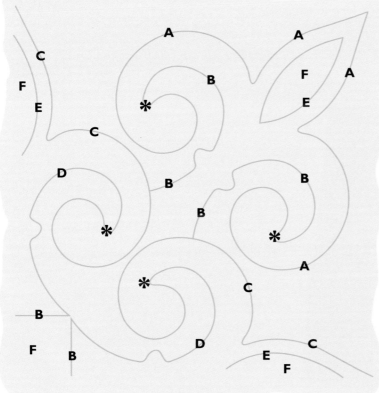

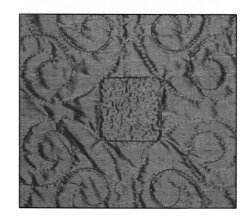

Cabled wall-hanging

This is a very easy-to-make project; the simple patchwork gives you the chance to try your new stitching on a traditional cabled quilting design. You can follow my stitching choices, or try your own variations – don't forget to balance your busy stitches with simpler ones.

Finished dimensions: 28in (65cm) square

✎ **Fabric requirements**
- 30in (75cm) main (dark) fabric
- 20in (50cm) sashing (lighter) fabric
- 31in (80cm) square of wadding
- 30in (75cm) backing fabric
- 20in (50cm) binding fabric

✎ **Additional requirements**
- Quilting thread and needle
- Quilting design or stencil

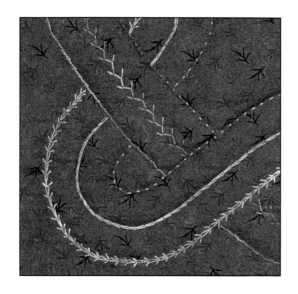

Cutting

- From the main (darker) fabric, cut:
  nine 7½in (19cm) squares
- From the sashing (lighter) fabric, cut:
  four strips measuring 2 x 27½in (5 x 70cm), and
  twelve strips measuring 2 x 7½in (5 x 19cm)

Construction

1 Join the blocks and short (vertical) sashing pieces into rows of three blocks and four sashings as shown in **a**. You will now have three rows as shown in **b**.

a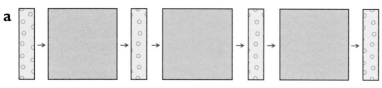

2 Now stitch all the long (horizontal) sashings between these rows (**c**) to form a nine-patch quilt.

b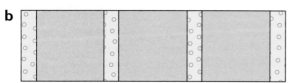

3 Prepare your backing fabric and lay it right side down on your work surface. Lay your wadding on top of the backing fabric. Give your quilt top one last press and lay this, right side up, on top of the wadding; tack a grid across the work (see page 128) to secure the three layers (**d**).

4 If you haven't done so by now, mark up your design on the quilt top (**e**). If you're using the designs provided, mark pattern A on the centre of the central square, pattern B onto each corner square, and pattern C onto each of the other four squares.

c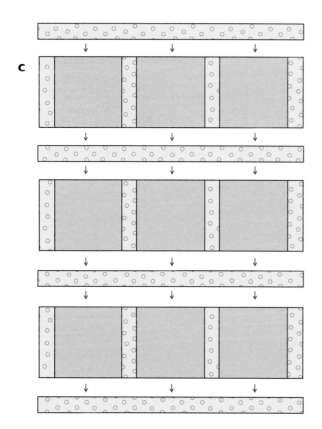

d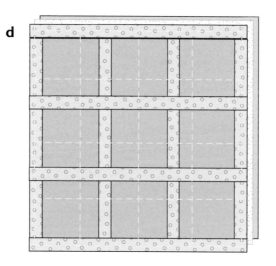

5 Quilt your design, either traditionally or using QWAD alternative stitches. (See the diagram on page 94 for the stitches used on my quilt; you can use the same ones if you like, or change them to suit yourself.) Begin with your central square, followed by the surrounding squares. Frame each individual square with a row of quilting.

6 When your quilting is finished, add the binding (see page 134), and remove the tacking (**f**).

You might like to label your quilt with your name and the date, or add a hanging sleeve or loops if it is to become a wall-hanging (see pages 137 and 138).

Pattern A

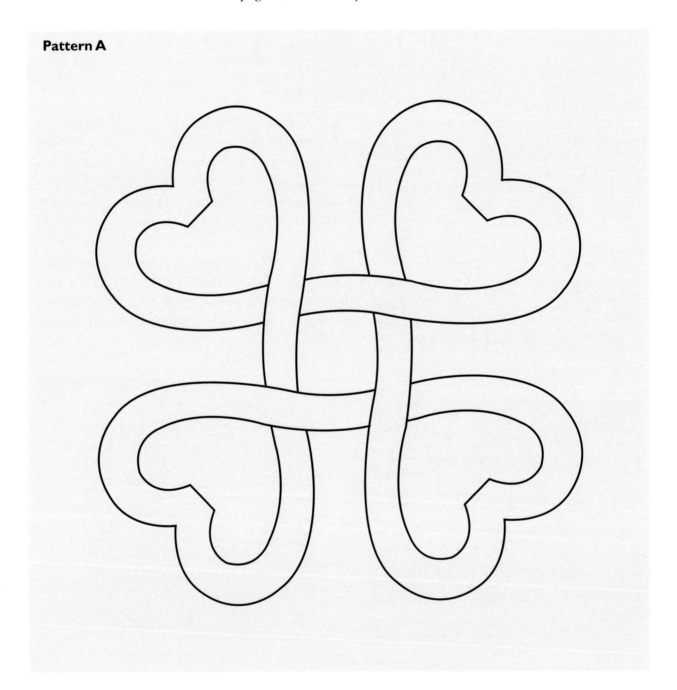

e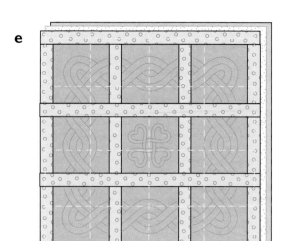

f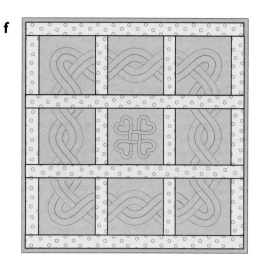

Pattern B

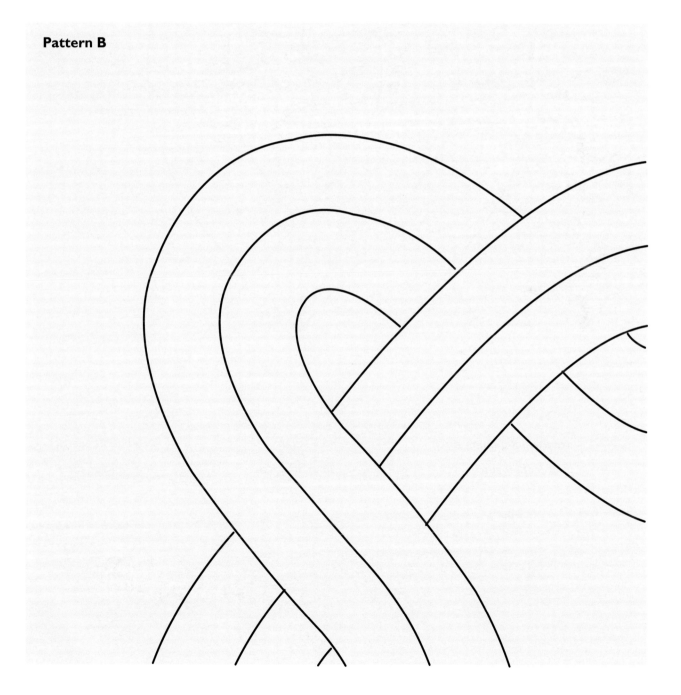

Pattern C

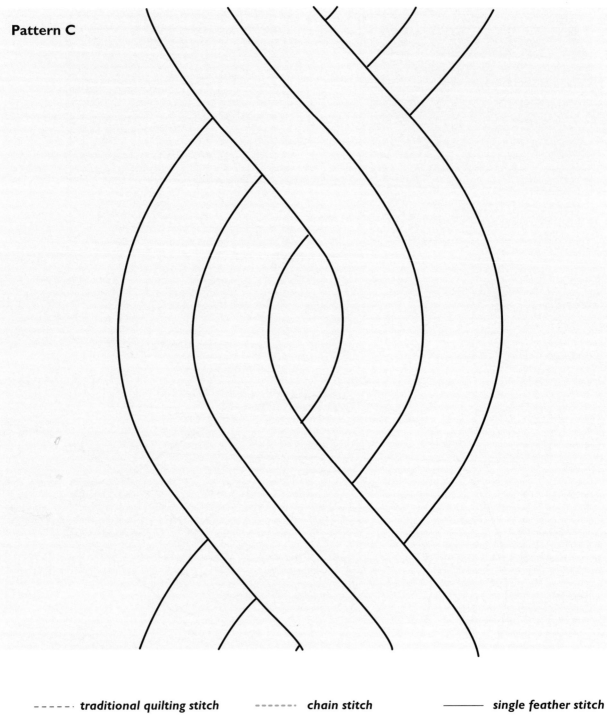

- - - - - *traditional quilting stitch*   - - - - - *chain stitch*   ———— *single feather stitch*

———— *half feather stitch*   - - - - - *wheatear stitch*   ———— *double knot stitch*

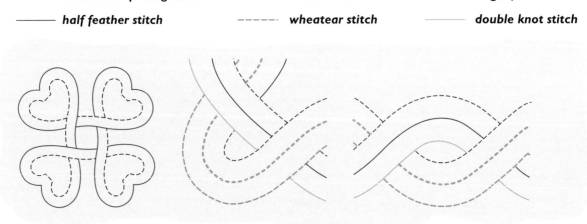

Sampler lap quilt

Give full rein to your alternative stitches on this lap quilt, which provides a perfect canvas for both traditional and stylised/freehand quilting designs. The patchwork piecing is very straightforward, consisting simply of squares and strips; if you've never made a quilt using the quilt-as-you-go method, now's your chance to try out the technique on a small, manageable project.

Finished dimensions: 31 in (71 cm) square

✎ Fabric requirements

- 22in square (or fat quarter-metre) of each of three green fabrics – one light, one mid-toned and one dark-toned

- 22in square (or fat quarter-metre) of each of three different prints:

    fabric A for sashings surrounding the dark green fabric
    fabric B for sashings surrounding the mid green fabric
    fabric C for sashings surrounding the light green fabric

- 39in (1m) of backing fabric

- 39in (1m) square of wadding

- 20in (50cm) of binding fabric

✎ **Additional requirements**

- Quilting design – see the different objects (page 98-99) that I've used for inspiration!
- Fabric-marker
- Quilting thread and needle

Cutting

Quilted squares

- From dark green fabric, cut: two 7½in (19cm) squares
- From mid green fabric, cut: four 7½in (19cm) squares
- From light green fabric, cut: three 7½in (19cm) squares

Sashings

- From fabric A, for the sashings surrounding the dark green squares, cut:
  four strips measuring 2 x 7½in (5 x 19cm)
  and four strips measuring 2 x 11½in (5 x 29cm)
- From fabric B, for the sashings surrounding the mid green squares, cut:
  eight strips measuring 2 x 7½in (5 x 19cm)
  and eight strips measuring 2 x 11½in (5 x 29cm)
- From fabric C, for the sashings surrounding the light green squares, cut:
  six strips measuring 2 x 7½in (5 x 19cm)
  and six strips measuring 2 x 11½in (5 x 29cm)

Wadding

- Cut nine squares of wadding, each measuring 13in (33cm) square

Backing fabric

- Cut nine squares of backing fabric, each measuring 13in (33cm) square

Construction

1 On one square of green fabric add two shorter sashing strips (one to each side, as shown in **a**), followed by two longer-length sashing strips (one at the top and and one at the bottom of the square, as shown in **b**). Repeat this process with each of the nine green squares, following the plan shown for positioning sashing fabrics A, B or C around the light, medium or dark green squares (**c**).

2 Layer each sashed square individually with a square of wadding and a square of backing fabric – the wadding and backing fabric should be slightly larger all round than the sashed square (**d**). Pin the layers of each individual fabric sandwich before tacking a grid (see page 128) to secure the layers ready for quilting (**e**). Remove the pins.

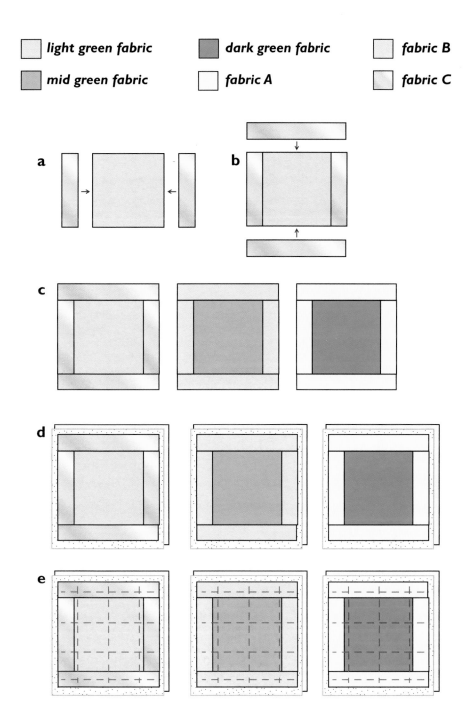

light green fabric   **dark green fabric**   **fabric B**

mid green fabric   **fabric A**   **fabric C**

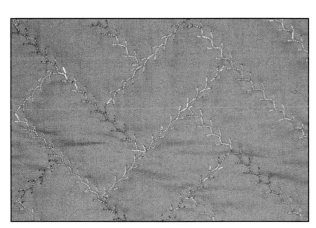

3 Quilt each square individually with a different design (see my notes and diagrams for design ideas and stitches – you can either use mine or create your own mixtures). Frame each green square with a row of quilting. Ensure that you keep the quilting within the green square and don't stitch further than ¼in (5mm) onto the sashings. (At the sashing edge, the three layers have to be kept free of quilting to enable you to join the squares using the quilt-as-you-go method.)

f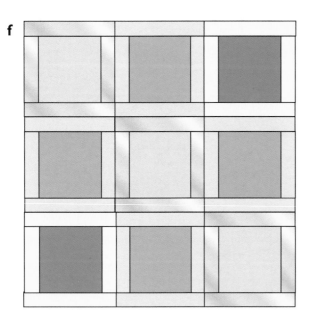

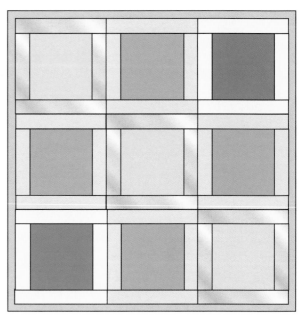 **g**

4 Follow the instructions on page 130 for the quilt-as-you-go method of construction; join the squares to create the layout shown in **f**. Once the centre of your quilt is put together, add the binding (see page 134) as shown in **g**; remove all the tacking threads and display your quilt. This is a stylised sampler which gives you the chance to create a unique quilt; use whatever you have to hand to draw round as guidelines for your designs. See what I've used for inspiration:

A Pattern 1 (opposite)
stitches used: double knot stitch

B The inner cut-out shape from my set square
stitches used: double knot stitch and traditional quilting stitch

C The rim of a saucer
stitches used: chain stitch

D Lines from my ruler, marked randomly
stitches used: open Cretan stitch, seeding

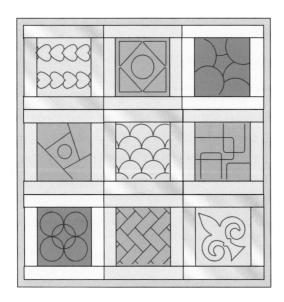

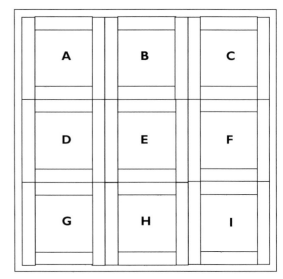

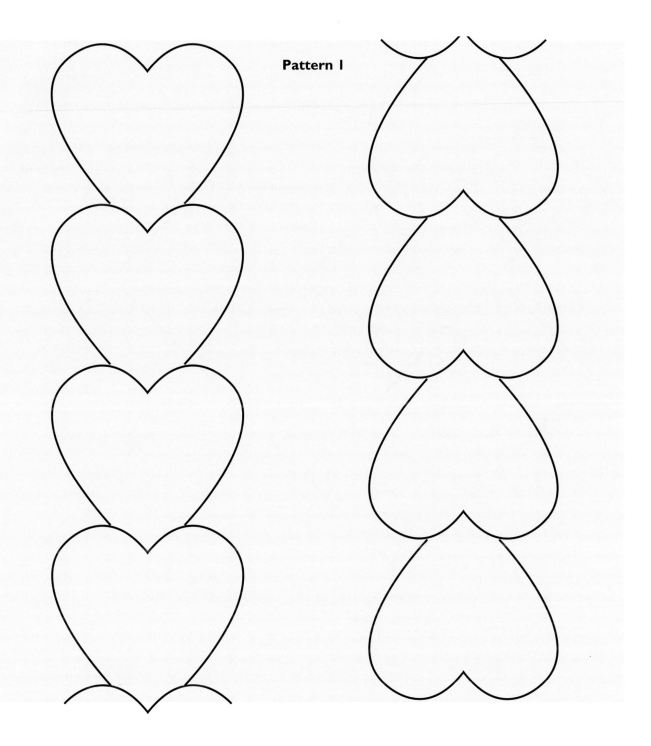

Pattern 1

E Part of pattern 3 (page 101)
  stitches used: traditional quilting stitch, threaded

F The outline of the packaging from a rotary cutter
  stitches used: chain stitch

G Reels of sticky tape, producing overlapping rings
  stitches used: chain stitch, whipped chain stitch

H Pattern 2 (page 100), used to create an infill/background design
  stitches used: single feather stitch

I Pattern 4 (page 102)
  stitches used: traditional quilting stitch, whipped

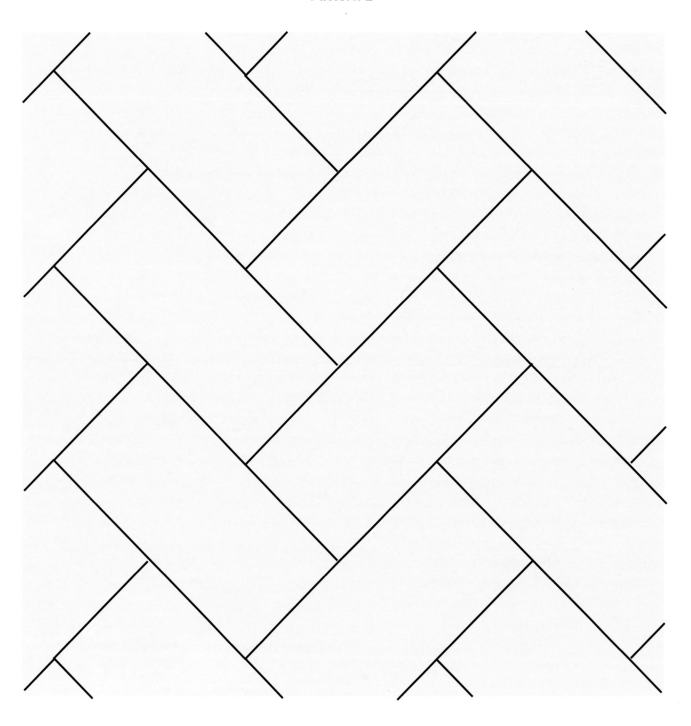

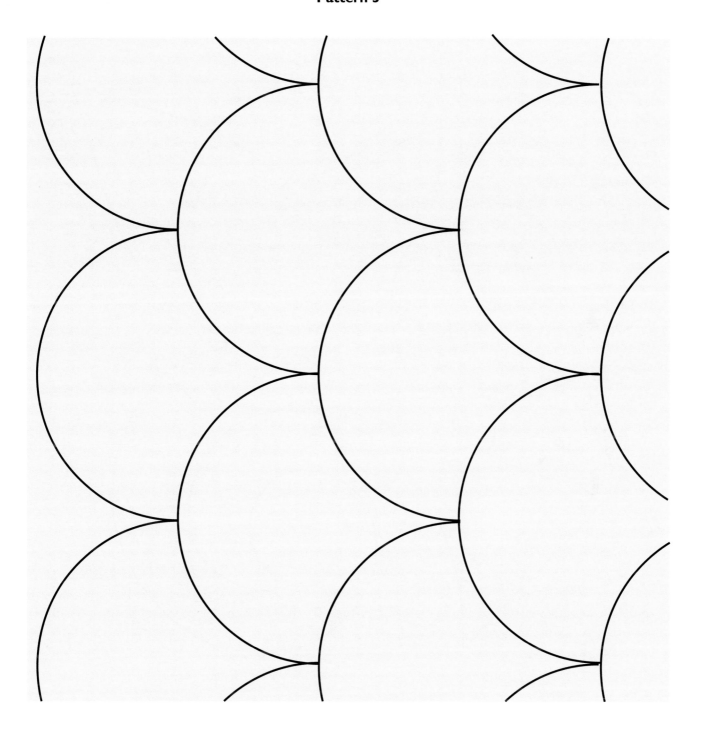

Shisha sampler

Shisha means 'little mirror'. Once you've practised and are confident embroidering your mirrors onto fabric, perhaps you'd like to make this eye-catching and twinkly wall-hanging. It's fun to make; you can use different methods of shisha embroidery and some lovely bright, rainbow-shaded threads. The mirror work is offset by traditional background quilting.

The random-pieced border is optional – you can use a plain border if you prefer, or make a wider one if you'd like a larger sampler. If you want to piece your binding, cut random lengths of fabric on the bias and join them to create further flashes of colour at the very edge of the hanging; this is a good way of using up any fabrics left over from the main project.

Finished dimensions: 21in (54cm) square

✎ Fabric requirements

For the mirrored squares
- Sixteen different squares of fabric, ranging in tonal value or colour (or a fat quarter-metre of one fabric of your choice)

For the sashing and backing (these use the same fabric)
- 39in (1m) of a contrast fabric or tartan/plaid
- 20in (50cm) of fabric for the binding (or scraps of fabrics joined on the cross/bias)
- 24in (60cm) square of of wadding

✎ Additional requirements
- Quilting stencil; you can either use the design shown (see diagram on page 108), or your own patterns
- Fabric-marker
- Quilting threads and needle
- Single-strand embroidery thread and embroidery needle
- 16 medium-sized shisha (mirrors)

My sample shows: Feather and cable designs stitched using traditional quilting thread in three different shades of pink. Shisha embroidered with hand-dyed, variegated silk thread.

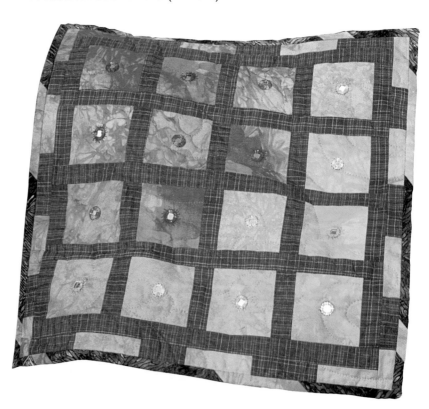

Cutting

- For the mirrored squares, cut:
  sixteen 3¾in (9.5cm) squares of fabric

- For the sashing, cut:
  two strips of fabric measuring the width of the fabric x 1½in (4cm) deep

  five strips of fabric measuring 19in (48cm) wide x 1½in (4cm) deep

Construction

1 If you're hand-piecing your patchwork, cut the longest strips of sashing into short pieces measuring 3¾in (9.5cm) each in length and add these to the sides of your main fabric squares (**a**). If you're machining, speed up this process by placing your main fabric squares along your strip of sashing fabric as shown in **b** – sew as many squares as you can fit along your sashing strip, but leave a little room between each to cut them apart easily (**c**). You'll need to use the full length of your first longest sashing strip, and only part of your second one – the surplus fabric will give you your extra sashings strips for the ends of the rows – see step 2.

2 Once you have all your squares with one piece of sashing added to each, press the sashings to one side, and then join these squares in a row so that you have four squares in a horizontal row with one sashing in between each square. Add one more sashing strip at the final end of each strip (**d**). Once you've constructed four horizontal rows like this, join them together with the remaining five pre-cut strips of sashing fabric to make your quilt top (**e**).

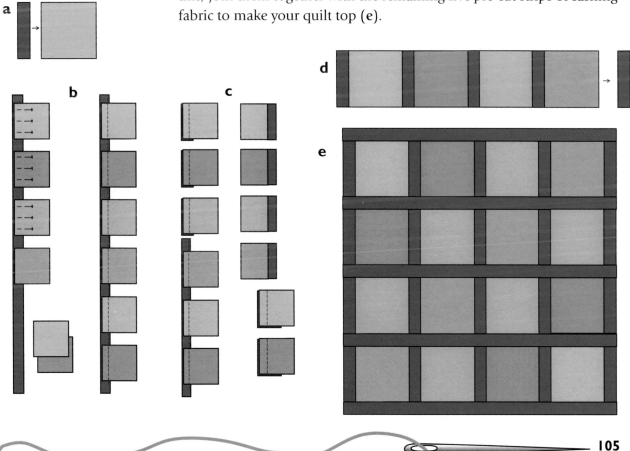

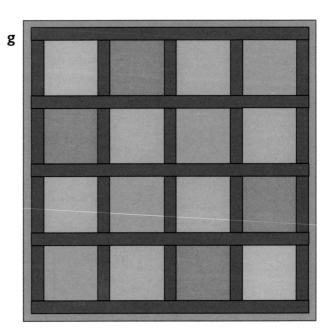

3 You can construct an optional border and add it at this stage if you like. Cut any surplus fabric into strips measuring 1½in (4cm) wide by random lengths, and join these together, either straight or at an angle (**f**), then add this border to the edges of your quilt. If you prefer, use a plain border (**g**).

4 Cut a piece of backing fabric and a piece of wadding to the same size as your quilt top; put the three layers together and sandwich with a grid of tacking (see page 128), as shown in **h**.

5 Choose a quilting design that complements the embellishment with shisha – I always prefer a flowing, curvilinear design rather than a geometric pattern. The pattern on page 108-109 is the one I used in my example; if you want to use it too, you can repeat the pattern in the layout shown on the right to cover your quilt.

6 You'll find it easier if you get your quilting completed first before embroidering the mirrors in place, but it is possible to do it the other way round if you prefer. Mark your quilting design (if you haven't already done this), then work your chosen quilting or QWAD stitches; follow any of the techniques shown on pages 74-76 for adding the shisha. Bind your quilt, remove the tacking threads and display (**i**).

h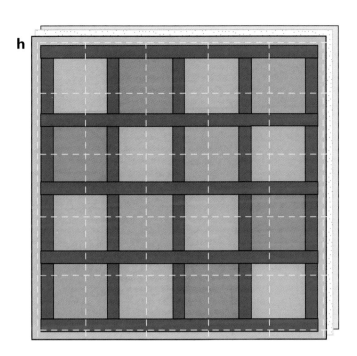

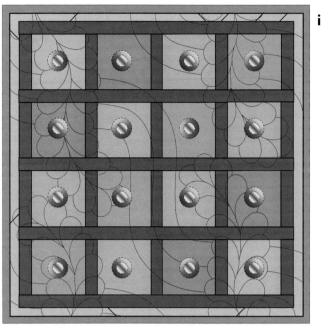 i

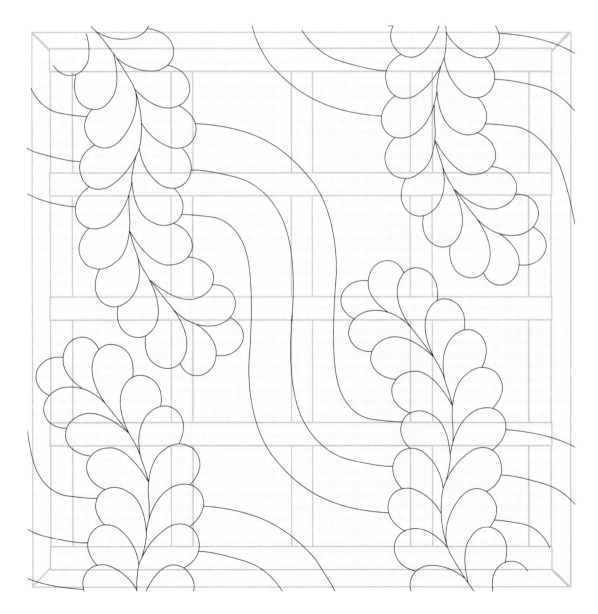

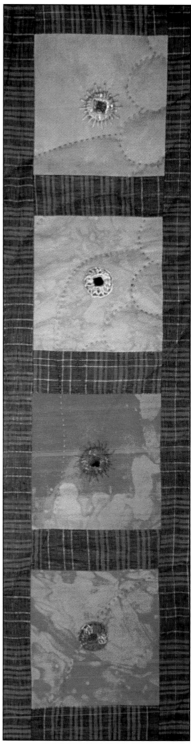

Small scatter cushions

Smaller cushions are easy to sew and can be completed in next to no time. Everyone likes to receive a gift with a personal touch – why not make some little cushions for friends or family? Add dried lavender for a herbal pillow, or add a stitched message on the front or back to make a special keepsake. Dimpling the centre with a button or decorative thread can add an extra dimension.

Dimensions of finished cushions: 10in (25cm) square and 10in (25cm) diameter

✎ Fabric requirements

For each cushion you will need:

- 10½in (27cm) square of marbled fabric for the cushion front
- 10½in (27cm) square of wadding
- 10½in (27cm) square of muslin
- 10½in (27cm) square of calico

✎ Additional requirements

- Quilting thread and needle
- Quilting design (page 113)
- 10in (25cm) cushion pad, either square or circular, or toy stuffing or scraps of wadding for stuffing

Instructions

1 Layer a square of top fabric, wadding and muslin and tack them together to form a fabric sandwich (see page 128).

2 Mark your quilting design on your top fabric, as shown in **a** (or do this before you layer, if you prefer). Use the design on page 113, which shows half of the full-size pattern.

3 Quilt your design using any of your preferred Quilting With A Difference stitches (see page 112 for the stitches I've used).

4 When your quilting is complete, lay your panel right side up on a flat work surface. Take your square of calico and lay this on top of your quilted panel. For the square cushion: stitch by machine around three complete sides of the square plus approximately 2in (5cm) in from each end of the fourth side (**b**). Clip the corners of the cushion cover (**c**), before turning it through to the right side (**d**), using the gap that you've left on the fourth side, and stuffing as on page 112 (**e**).

f

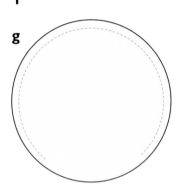

g

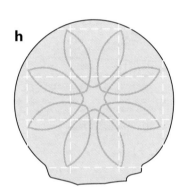

h

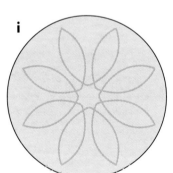

i

5 For the round cushion: mark a circle on your calico (try using a saucer or dish as a template), then stitch around this circle by machine, leaving approximately 4in (10cm) unstitched for a turning hole (**f**). Clip the seam allowance back to a scant quarter inch (**g**) before turning the cushion through to the right side (**h**), using the gap you've left unstitched.

6 Remove all the tacking from your cushion panel. Use the cushion pad, toy stuffing or scraps of wadding to fill out your cushion; if you're using dried lavender, add it to the stuffing at this stage. Fold under the raw edges of the turning opening, and slip-stitch closed (**i**).

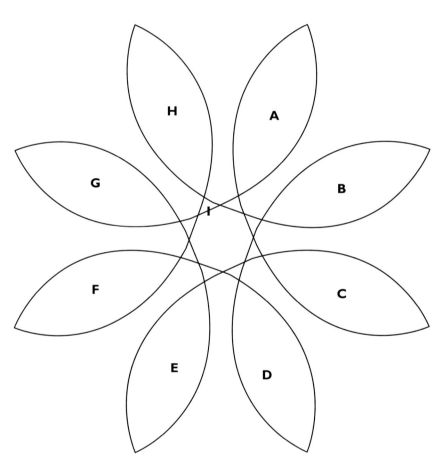

I used these stitches in this arrangement on the square green cushion; the circular cushion and the panels for the wall-hanging (see pages 114-115) feature the same stitches but in different arrangements.

A running stitch – threaded or whipped   **F** fly stitch
B herringbone   **G** whipped chain stitch
C chain stitch   **H** open chain stitch
D fern stitch   **I** running stitch to link the 'petals'
E blanket stitch

Three-panel hanging

If you enjoyed making the small scatter cushions, perhaps you'd like to use the same basic squares to create this cheery and easy-to-sew wall-hanging. You can use two, three, four, or even more panels.
If you join them with buttons or cords, they can be rearranged from time to time to ring the changes – or use 'S' hooks and an attractive wire quilt hanger as I've done here.

- *Finished dimensions: approx. 9½ x 28½in (24 x 72.5cm)*

✎ Fabric requirements

- Three 9in (23cm) squares of marbled fabric
- Three 9in (23cm) squares of wadding
- Three 9in (23cm) squares of backing fabric
- 22in square (or fat quarter-metre) of binding fabric

✎ Additional requirements

- Quilting thread and needle
- Additional scraps of fabric for (optional) hanging loops
- Twelve ¾in (17mm) buttons
- Four metal S hooks (see Suppliers on page 143)
- Wire quilt hanger (optional)

Cutting

- From the binding fabric, cut:

  six widths from the 22in square or fat quarter, each one measuring 21½in (55cm) x 3½in (9cm) deep

- from each of these strips, cut one piece measuring 9in (22cm) – the remaining longer strip can be used for the longer edge of your binding.

Construction

1 Follow steps 1–3 for the construction of the small scatter cushions (see page 111), but make three panels, either all the same or different. Choosing your favourite Quilting With A Difference stitches, or following my stitch plan as before, quilt your design/s.

2 Treat each panel as a small quilt and add quilt binding to each (see page 134), as shown in **a**. Remove all the tacking threads.

3 Sew a button to each corner of the three panels (**b**), then either link the panels with decorative cords or threads or use the metal S hooks (**c**). (If you prefer, you could omit the buttons and loops and just slip-stitch the three panels together at the binding, as shown in **d**.) Finish off the display if you wish by adding hanging loops to the top panel and using a wire quilt hanger (**e**).

• *Cinnamon Twist*

26½in (67cm) square

A play with circles within squares and tonal values, this quilt incorporates many textured fibres including cottons, silks, velvets, chamois leather, towelling and broderie anglaise. The whole piece was hand-quilted throughout, using space-dyed silk threads with featured areas of seeding.

• *Masquerade*

66in (168cm) wide, 55in (140cm) deep

Stitches used on Masquerade

Stitches used on Masquerade

on the borders:

double knot stitch

whipped running stitch

chain stitch

traditional quilting with both silk and cotton threads

single feather stitch

on the central panel:

single feather stitch

Vandyke stitch

fern stitch

double knot stitch

closed blanket stitch

wheatear stitch

zigzag chain stitch

traditional chain stitch

whipped chain stitch

shisha work

plus traditional quilting as an infill to the background

Initially planned as a further teaching sample for Quilting With A Difference, this piece grew and designed itself into a full-blown quilt (I find that most quilts will design themselves onwards and upwards if allowed …). I see this work as patchwork masquerading as wholecloth – contemporary work masquerading as traditional. The fabrics I used are commercially-printed cottons, with batiks for the staggered prairie point edging, and couched 'piping' made from ripped fabric strips.

Masquerade is hand-quilted throughout using both traditional quilting thread and hand-dyed silk threads; I used Quilting With A Difference 'alternative' stitching (see left) and traditional quilting, adding further embellishment with embroidered shisha and beading.

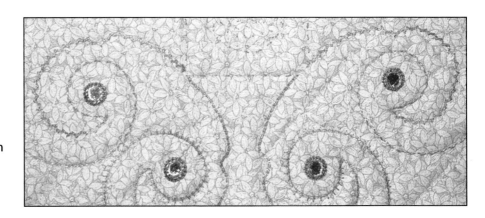

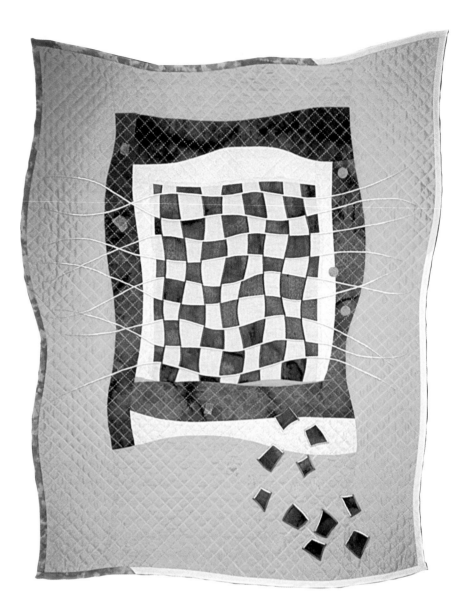

• Mint Julep

34in (86cm) wide, 41in (104cm) deep

During 2001, I spent some time experimenting with gridded patchwork – a step back to some earlier quilts that I'd particularly enjoyed making (*Imagine*, 1997, and *Imagine: Another Dimension,* 1998). My love of all things geometric lends itself well to grids, and many of my quilts show a grid of some sort, often cross-hatched or overlaid with a curvilinear design.

Mint Julep was constructed by cutting and weaving two fabrics onto a Vilene base and stablising them with machine appliqué. Freehand-cut curves (used throughout) were surprisingly easy both to cut and to sew. The techniques I used include machine appliqué (extended to the borders), machine quilting on the centre, and cross-hatched hand-quilting in space-dyed threads throughout the double border.

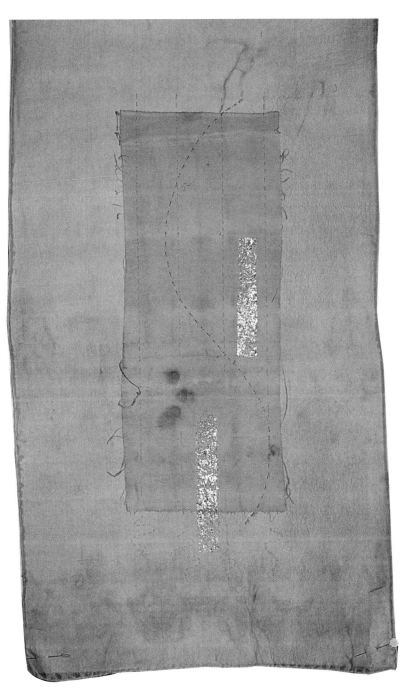

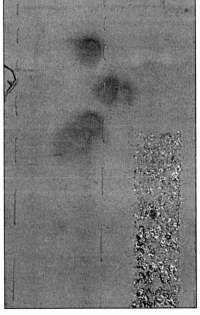

• *Rainfall at Giverny*

12in (31cm) wide, 27in (69cm) long

Pieces of habotai and noile silks (hand-dyed using colours remaining from other projects) were used to construct this mounted textile piece. I've incorporated panels of bonding-web printed with metallic foil. The whole piece is hand-quilted onto a base of pelmet Vilene using dyed silk thread and copper wire.

Stitches used on
3 into 2 Will Go
traditional quilting
seeding
knotting and tufting
sword-edged stitch
star filling stitch
fly stitch
daisy stitch

3 into 2 Will Go

23in (59cm) square

In 2001, the Quilters' Guild of the British Isles Region 2 requested 24in (61cm) square quilts for a second travelling suitcase exhibition. The theme was 'Region 2.' I returned to a previous quilt that I'd designed (*Reflections*, 1997), and worked a further interpretation using the Quilters' Guild colours and bringing in a play on the logos of both the Guild and the Region (three rings representing the counties of Kent, Surrey and Sussex).

I worked 'alternative' stitches in a cream flower thread, using the different stitches and the various textured fabrics to reflect the diverse talents to be found among the region's quilters. The techniques also include curved-seam patchwork and hand- and machine-quilting. The reverse side shows reverse (!) appliqué and couched trapunto wool. Apart from the traditional quilting, I used all the other stitches randomly as filling stitches.

• Sea Urchins

35in (89cm) wide, 49in (125cm) deep

Following on from *Mint Julep*, this quilt was actually pieced
(rather than woven) using traditional patchwork piecing and
freehand drawn templates, with further freehand-cut curves
(a technique I also used for piecing the backing). The fabrics
include commercial cottons and silks. I hand-quilted this
project throughout with space-dyed silk threads and hand-
embroidered shisha (mirrors).

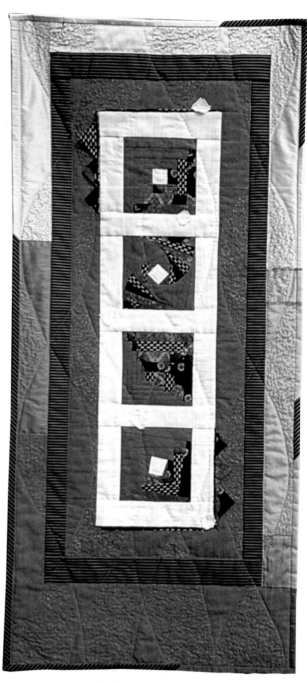

•Sugar and Spice

24in (61cm) wide, 49½in (126cm) deep

Sugar and Spice originally started life as four teaching samples for my Learn About Log Cabin workshop. Because I loved the mix of oriental and western fabrics and the mixed textures (silks, cottons – even a too-good-to-miss selvedge was used), the samples actually 'grew up' to become a quilt. This piece is hand-quilted throughout, using hand-dyed silk threads alongside cotton sashiko thread (for both traditional quilting and large areas of seeding).

back to basics

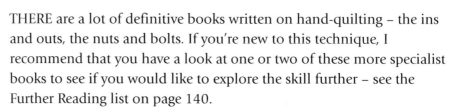

Quilting

Introducing hand-quilting

If you're stuck for ideas on a colour-scheme, nature has an endless selection to choose from. You could use subtle colours, along the lines of the wisteria plant below or the foliage at the top of page 125, or bright and contrasting ones, such as the lupins opposite or the shrub at the bottom of this page.

THERE are a lot of definitive books written on hand-quilting – the ins and outs, the nuts and bolts. If you're new to this technique, I recommend that you have a look at one or two of these more specialist books to see if you would like to explore the skill further – see the Further Reading list on page 140.

More than just a running stitch …

I THINK it's important not to dismiss hand-quilting simply as a 'running-stitch.' Although it is the same in appearance, there's a lot more to it than that – which becomes apparent when you realise that you have to secure three layers, including a wadding, with each stitch.

Ideally, hand-quilting stitches will look the same on the back of the work as on the front – this isn't always the case, especially when you're hand-quilting through patchwork seams and junctions, with increased bulk at those points. It's important to try to achieve neat and even stitching, and you'll find this easier if you aim to take several stitches on your needle at a time rather than single stitches (this is far easier to do when you're sewing a straight line, and almost impossible when you're stitching a tight curve).

Quality, not quantity

YOU'LL always be told about the quilter who can sew 20 stitches to the inch – I'm sure she's out there somewhere, but no-one I know has ever met her! It's preferable to take slightly larger quilt stitches and sew them evenly, rather than create tiny, randomly-placed stitches. (And please avoid individual stab-stitching like the plague! This is the technique of taking your needle down through the work and pushing it back up through the quilt in a separate movement. Not only will it take you a lifetime to quilt your quilt – the stitching on the back of the project will invariably be uneven.)

One thing worth remembering is that it's difficult to take a small stitch with a big needle. Try starting with one of the larger quilting needles from a mixed pack, and set yourself the challenge of working down

through the sizes. You may find it impossible to use the smallest-sized needle if you're lap quilting, as there is virtually nothing to grip with your finger and thumb. These tiny-sized needles are generally aimed at quilters who use a quilt frame or hoop, where there is a considerable difference in technique.

Don't be intimidated by other people's work; when viewed as a whole, your stitching will take on a more even appearance than when you are scrutinizing each stitch in close detail.

My instructions are given for 'lap quilting' – that is, hand-quilting without the use of a quilt frame or hoop. This is my preferred method of quilting and the one which works best with Quilting With A Difference. If you prefer to try hand-quilting with a quilt frame or hoop, I suggest that you invest in a workshop with a good tutor who can show you how to do this properly.

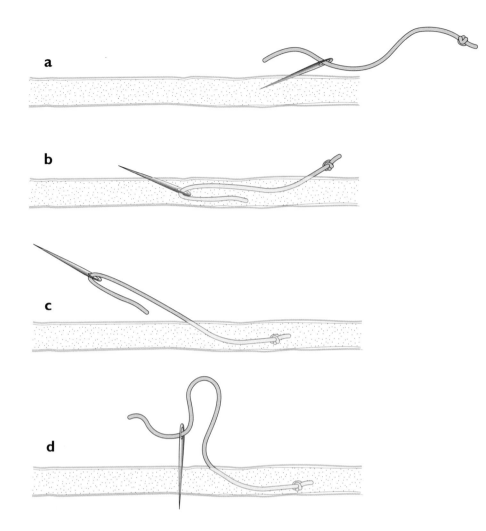

Hand-quilting: the basics

1 Mark your design onto the fabric and layer your sandwich (see page 128). (The design can be marked after the sandwich is layered if you prefer, though some marking methods are easier to do before sandwiching.)

2 Choose your quilting needle. Specialised quilting needles are called Betweens. The higher the number of the needle, the smaller the needle itself is; and the smaller the needle, the smaller the stitch!

3 Now choose your quilting thread and cut a length; ideally, keep the length to 18in maximum. Make a neat knot in one end, then insert the needle into the quilt top about a needle's length away from the starting point for your stitching (**a**). Pass your needle through the top fabric and wadding only until it surfaces at your starting point (**b**), then gently pull the thread to pop your knot into the wadding to hold it secure (**c**).

4 Working always from the surface of your project, begin by taking the first stitch with your needle virtually perpendicular (at right angles) to your work (**d**) – if you can make this stitching angle quite acute each time your needle goes down into the work, you'll find you have more success with securing the backing fabric.

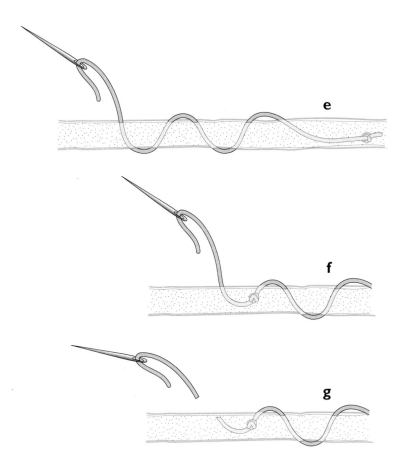

Take several stitches through the three layers and back to the surface (**e**); once you have this technique up and running, you'll find that your hand has a rocking motion while stitching.

5 Pull the needle through the fabric; don't be tempted to pull the thread tight – just pull it through enough for the stitches to lie flat on the fabric and no more. Continue in the same way all around your marked design, preferably starting near the centre and working outwards.

6 To finish off a thread, make a neat knot in it about one stitch length away from your fabric; take a further stitch if you have room (a back stitch if not), and run the needle through the top fabric and wadding only (**f**). Once more, pop your knot through the top fabric into the wadding, then snip off the remaining tail of thread (**g**). You should end up with neat work back and front, no knots visible.

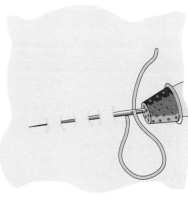

If you're quilting with a hoop, the project in the frame needs to have some give or slack – it doesn't need to be drumskin tight. The needle isn't actually gripped between finger and thumb while you're stitch-making, as it is with lap quilting; it's only gripped when the needle is first pushed into the fabric and then again when it's pulled through. While you're making the stitches, the eye of the needle rests in the dimples of your thimble (**h**) and your pushing finger works alone, rocking the needle. Once again, all your stitching should be sewn from the surface of the work.

Tacking a fabric 'sandwich'

Why tack?

BEFORE you quilt, the three layers of your project (quilt top, wadding and backing) have to be secured so that they don't move or distort while you're quilting. There are various methods of doing this; the most common is tacking, or basting, which involves making lines of large holding stitches across the project. The lines of tacking will be removed once the project is quilted, so do use up any old thread which you don't use any more for sewing, or treat yourself to a large, economy cone of thread (you can pick these up at any major quilt show if your local shop doesn't have them).

Tacking can be tedious, but a well-tacked quilt will make the whole quilting process quicker, and a lot more enjoyable. Here are some tips for successful tacking:

| Lay the backing fabric on a flat surface, right side down, and smooth it out. Cover this with the wadding, then lay the quilt top, right side up, on top of the wadding. Pin the layers together, but sparsely – just a few pins here and there to hold the layers (**a**).

> When you're using tacking stitches a larger-than-usual needle will speed things up – remember, tacking is a means to an end and will eventually be taken out. It's an important job and one worth doing properly, but it doesn't have to look good!

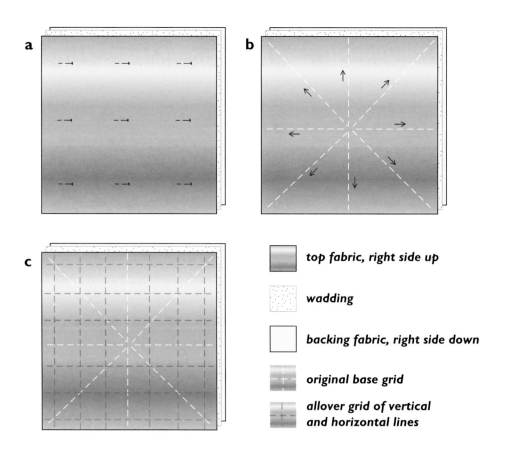

top fabric, right side up

wadding

backing fabric, right side down

original base grid

allover grid of vertical and horizontal lines

2 Tack the lines of your first, base grid from the centre outwards; tack the diagonals and the horizontal and vertical half-way lines (**b**). You might find it to use 'teaspoon tacking' – see below. (Don't be tempted to tack a line of stitching all the way round the outer edge; if you do this, you'll prevent the three layers from travelling outwards evenly when the quilting is in progress.) Remove the pins.

3 Now tack the overall grid. Working by eye, work lines of tacking approximately 2-3in (5-8cm) apart on a small project such as a cushion panel or small hanging, 3-4in (8-10cm) on a larger quilt (**c**).

Teaspoon tacking

HAVE the tacking needle in your sewing hand and a teaspoon in your

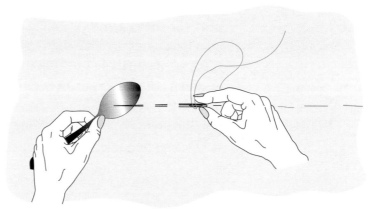

other hand; when you take the point of the needle down through the fabric layers and bring it up to the surface again, run the point of the needle into the bowl of the teaspoon instead of trying to grab at it with your finger and thumb, then pull the needle and thread through with your sewing hand. This will speed your tacking up considerably; the project will stay flatter on your work surface, and you won't be slowed down by worrying about pricking your fingers. Though it's useful on even the smallest project, you'll particularly benefit from teaspoon tacking when you're layering a larger quilt.

Alternatives to tacking

THERE are several alternative ways of holding the layers of your quilt sandwich together; these include:
- quilters' special safety pins (often quite large and curved)
- a small machine designed to shoot plastic kimbles or staples through the layers
- fusible or iron-on wadding
- special quilt glue

Joining quilt-as-you-go blocks

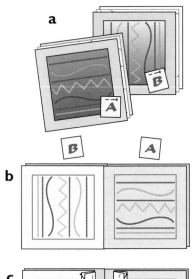

IF you've quilted a series of blocks individually, rather than joining the blocks into a complete quilt top, you'll need to use this method to join your quilted panels.

1 Lay your blocks out on a flat surface, then shuffle them around to find the best arrangement. Once you've decided on your layout, pin a number or letter to each block in sequence (**a**), so that you can stack them ready for construction.

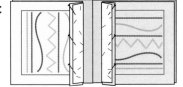

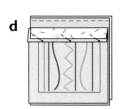

2 Take the first two blocks to be joined, and lay them face down, with the edges to be joined together (double-check this; it's easy to go wrong here!), as shown in **b**. (Note; the edges with short sashing strips are the first ones to be joined.) Pin the backing fabric and wadding out of the way on each block (**c**).

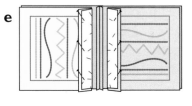

3 Pin and sew the seam to join the sashing (**d**), then finger-press this seam open (**e**).

4 Cut a piece of sturdy card to fit this section of your work and lay the card in place on top of the seam (**f**). (The card will prevent you from accidentally cutting the front of your work when you trim the wadding.) Unpin the wadding (leave the backing fabric pinned out of the way), and bring the two pieces of wadding down over the card so that they overlap (**g**). With scissors, cut right up the centre of the overlapped wadding and discard the surplus; you now have two pieces of wadding butting up perfectly to each other (**h**). Whipstitch the two edges together with generous stitches (**i**).

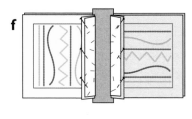

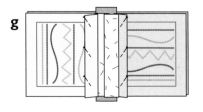

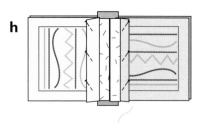

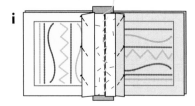

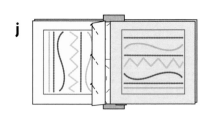

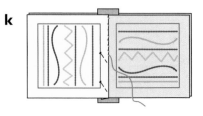

5 Leaving the card in place, unpin the backing fabric, and bring one section of it down so that it lies flat (**j**). Bring the other section down on top and fold the raw edge underneath; slipstitch this into place (**k**), and remove the card.

6 Once two blocks have been joined, you can re-tack and quilt the short sashings between them; if you do this as you go along, it's not quite such a daunting task as if you leave it all to the end. Leave the outer (long) sashing strips unquilted at this stage.

7 Join all the blocks in the same way, working first of all in pairs (**l**), so that you're working on small units as much as possible, and adding extra quilting as you go. Then join the pairs into strips (**m**)and so on to create the whole quilt (**n**); finally, bind it (**o**). (If you want to add a border, you should sandwich and quilt this first, then join it to the quilt top using the technique described above.)

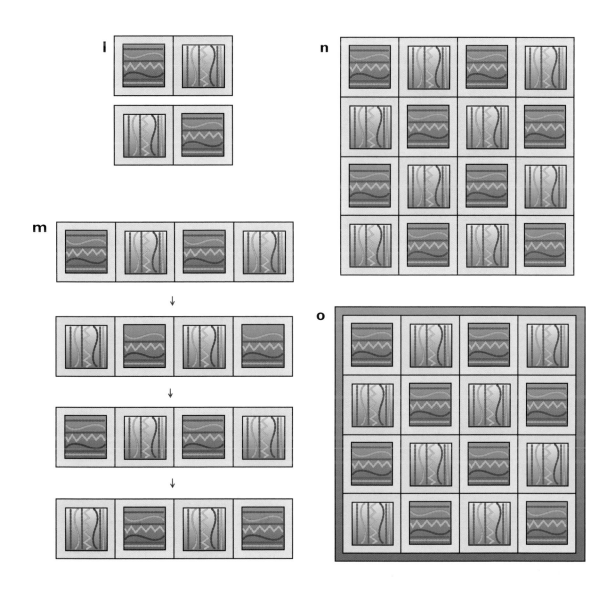

Quick and easy cushion covers

CUSHIONS make speedy and simple projects; here's an easy method for turning a quilted panel into a cushion cover, with no soft furnishing skills required!

The overlap of backing fabric should preferably be somewhere between 3in and 5in (roughly between 8 and 13cm). If the overlap is any smaller it will result in the opening gaping; if it's any larger, you may find it difficult to insert the cushion pad. Try the pieces out on your cushion panel, and trim the raw edges if the overlap is too big.

1 Once you've quilted your cushion cover design, leave some lines of basic tacking in place to secure the three layers, and trim the panel to square it up if necessary (**a**).

2 Measure one side of your square, then cut two rectangles of backing fabric the same depth as your square by two thirds of that measurement (**b**).

3 Neaten the two long edges that will remain visible, either by cutting your fabric so that these two edges are fabric selvedge, or by folding under a double hem and top-stitching it in place (**c**).

4 Place your quilted cushion panel right side down on your work surface, and lay one of the backing rectangles, right side up, on top, so that the raw edges align (**d**).

5 Place the second piece of backing fabric on top of this, right side up, so that the raw edges align and the two finished edges overlap (**e**)

a

b two-thirds of the cushion depth

depth of the cushion

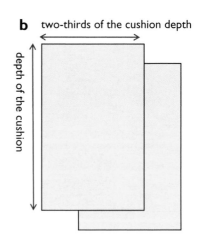

6 Pin all the way around the outer edge of the layered pieces – pin particularly securely where the two backing panels overlap (**f**).

7 Now turn the project right side up and bind the layers (**g**) with your chosen fabric in the same way as you would a quilt (see page 134); reinforce the areas where the backing fabric overlaps with an extra line of stitching.

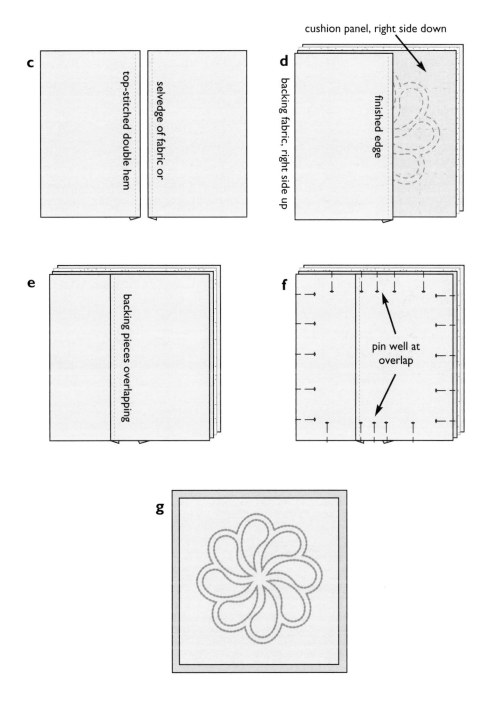

Finishing

Binding your quilt

1 To calculate the amount of fabric you need to bind your quilt, first of all measure all sides of the quilt. Then measure the width of your chosen binding fabric. Calculate how many widths of the fabric will be required for both the top and bottom edges and two sides of your quilt (this is more economical than buying the length of fabric required). Multiply this measurement by approximately 3in (8cm) – or however wide you want the binding strip to be – and this will give you your fabric requirement.

2 Cut strips of fabric across the width of your fabric by 3in (8cm) deep (**a**). Join any strips where necessary to achieve the final lengths required (one length for each of the four sides of your quilt), pressing the seams open to reduce the bulk (**b**).

3 Fold the prepared binding strips in half down their length and press (**c**).

4 Take one length of binding for one of the long sides of your quilt. Place it on the top of the quilt with the raw edges alongside the raw edges of your quilt top; pin it in place (**d**). Machine sew approximately ½in (1cm) in from the raw edges (**e**).

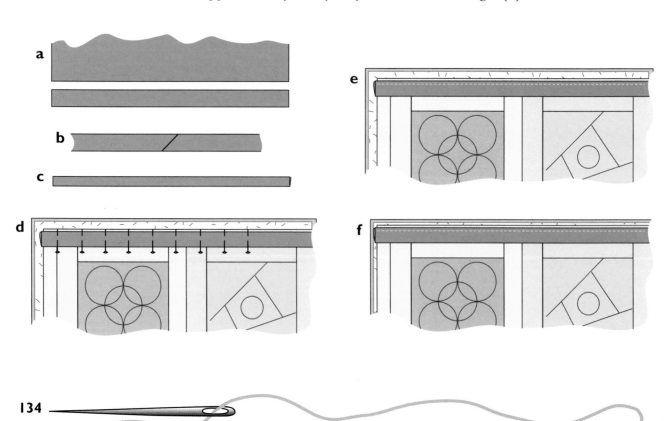

5 At this stage, trim back any surplus wadding and backing fabric so that it's very slightly larger than the quilt top (**f**); this helps to pad your binding out a little.

6 Push the folded edge of the binding to the back of the quilt and slipstitch it in place (**g**), covering the line of machine stitching.

7 Repeat on the opposite side of the quilt, and cut all the ends of the binding flush with the ends of the quilt top (**h**).

8 Repeat the process with the top and bottom edges of the quilt, but this time ensure that you leave at least 1-2in (3-5cm) of excess fabric overhanging each end (**i**). Machine your binding in place, then fold the excess flaps of fabric inwards as you turn the binding to the back of the quilt. As you slipstitch the binding on the back, slipstitch the ends closed at the corners of the quilt (**j**).

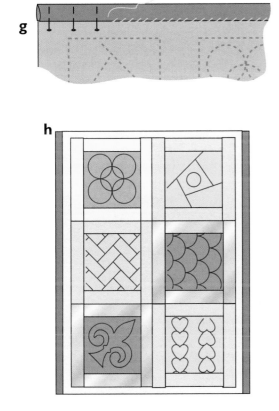

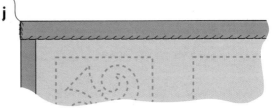

Easy label making

THIS is the easiest way to make a label for your quilt project.

1 Cut a piece of pale-coloured, plain fabric slightly larger than you want your finished label to measure; fuse a piece of lightweight iron-on interfacing to the back of the fabric to stabilise it (**a**).

2 Using a water-soluble fabric-marking pen and a ruler, draw in guidelines – the outer edges of your label, followed by some horizontal lines ready to take your written details (**b**).

3 Now use permanent fabric-marking pens to write the label details; these can include your name, the recipient's name, the date, a message, names of any patchwork blocks or fabric used, and the name of the quilt if it has one (**c**).

4 Using a pair of pinking shears, cut away the label following the blue pen guidelines for the outline (**d**). The interfacing and the pinked edge will prevent the edges of the label from fraying. Use a barely damp cotton-wool bud to blot away any blue pen lines that are left; do this gently so that you don't alter the surface of the fabric.

5 Using a decorative thread (and a decorative stitch if you wish), hand-sew the label to the back of your quilted project, stitching about ½in or 1cm in from the pinked edge (**e**). Make sure that you only catch the label and the backing fabric of your quilt with your stitching.

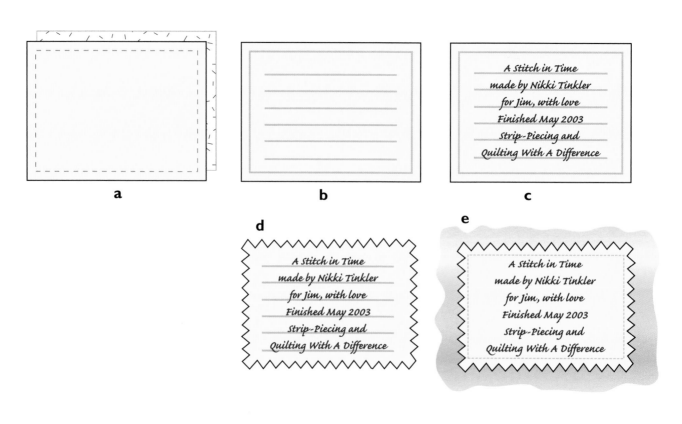

a   b   c

d   e

A Stitch in Time
made by Nikki Tinkler
for Jim, with love
Finished May 2003
Strip-Piecing and
Quilting With A Difference

Making a hanging sleeve

FOR a hanging sleeve, use either the same fabric as your quilt backing, or some leftover fabric from another project – calico is fine.

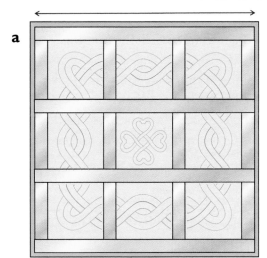

1 Measure the width of your project from just within the binding on one edge to just within the binding at the other (**a**). This is the length of your hanging sleeve. Cut a piece of fabric measuring this length by approximately 5in (12cm) wide, plus added seam allowance all round (**b**).

2 Turn under the raw edges on all sides of this fabric strip and top-stitch them to secure them (**c**)

3 Position the hanging sleeve on the back of your quilt so that it sits within the binding; pin it in position (**d**), and slip-stitch the top of the sleeve to the quilt backing (**e**).

4 Push the sleeve fabric up by about ½in (1cm) before you pin and slip-stitch the bottom edge (**f**); this will allow some 'give' to accommodate a hanging pole or batten.

An alternative method is to make a complete tube of fabric and attach it to your quilt in the same way (**g**); this will protect your quilt fabric and its stitching from any damage that might be caused by the actual insertion of the pole.

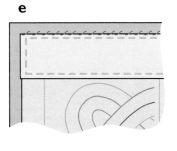

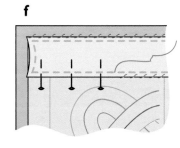

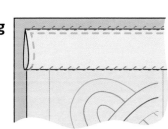

Display loops

Hanging loops are simple to make and can be an added feature of your project when you display it. If you're using loops it's best to add them while you're attaching the final edge of binding to your quilt, so that the raw edges of the loops can be incorporated into the binding.

I Stitch a tube of fabric (**a**) and turn it right side out (**b**). To save time, you can stitch one long tube, turn it out the right way, and then cut it into lengths (**c**). The length of each loop needs to be double the length you want to appear above your quilt, plus extra for seam allowances at each end (**d**).

2 Once your loops are right side out, position them along the top edge of your quilt at equal intervals and pin them in place (**e**). Once you've positioned them, incorporate the raw ends into the binding to create a neat finish (**f**).

> The number of hanging loops you need will depend on how wide your project is. By the same token, the size and width of your project will determine how wide you want your hanging loops to be. It's not a good idea to have delicate hanging loops on a large, heavy quilt; try to achieve a good balance between the two.

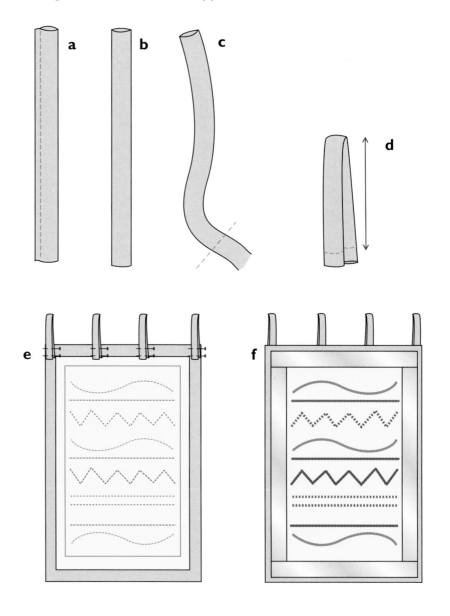

Taking things further

Research

If you'd like to discover more about hand-quilting, try researching these different areas

- contour quilting and echo quilting
- tie quilting – knotting and tufting
- sashiko (Japanese quilting)
- kantha (Indian quilting)
- Italian (corded) quilting
- trapunto (stuffed) quilting
- shadow quilting
- wholecloth/Durham quilting

Further reading

Good Housekeeping Embroidery ISBN 0 85223 201 2

Starting to Stitch Creatively ISBN 0 7063 6303 5

Anchor Book of Freestyle Embroidery Stitches ISBN 0 7153 0629 4

Mary Thomas's Dictionary of Embroidery Stitches, new edition by Jan Eaton ISBN 0 340 51075 7

Hand Quilting by Alex Anderson, C&T Publishing

Both the Quilters' Guild (see details below) and the Embroiderers' Guild have a list of relevant books available direct from them, either to borrow or to buy

UK magazines/publications

Patchwork and Quilting

Popular Patchwork

Fabrications

Magic Patch

The Quilter (Quilters' Guild members' magazine)

UK organisations

The Quilters' Guild of the British Isles, Room 190, Dean Clough, Halifax, West Yorkshire HX3 5AX (tel 01422 347669)
The British Quilt Study Group (contact via the Quilters' Guild, above)
The Quilt Association (tel 01686 413467)

UK exhibitions

The National Quilt Championships
The Spring and Autumn Quilt Festivals
Quilts UK
The Great Northern Quilt Show
The Scottish Quilt Championships
The South West Quilt Show
(contact Grosvenor Exhibitions Ltd, tel 01775 722900)

The Quilters' Guild of the British Isles annual show
The Quilters' Guild Region 2 annual autumn exhibition at Hever Castle (contact the Guild; see details above)

Photo: Jade Tinkler

Well, you've reached the end of my book; I hope you've enjoyed reading, stitching and experimenting for yourself. If you'd like to follow up the book with a little personal workshop exclusive to you, my video on this technique is also available. If you want to have a one-to-one chat, don't forget that you can e-mail me, either directly, or via my website address.

On the website you'll also find details of classes and workshops, talks on offer, and demonstration venues that I'll be attending.

I travel extensively, visiting groups and quilt shops who are interested in my work, and also demonstrating at quilt and needlecraft exhibitions. My world of quilting continues to present me with opportunities to visit places on the map that I've never been to before and perhaps would never have visited otherwise, with the added bonus of meeting so many wonderful, like-minded people (along with those who are just curious!).

If you're attending one of the quilt shows I might just be there – come and say hello, and take a closer look at my own Quilting With A Difference.

With best wishes

Nikki

e-mail: nikki@jtinkler.freeserve.co.uk
website: www.nikkitinkler.com

Acknowledgements

My chance to say thanks to all of the following special people:

*   Jim Tinkler, my husband, without whom none of my work would be possible
*   our son and daughter, Stephen and Jade, for making everything worthwhile
*   Tina and John Sellen, my parents, who always believed there was 'a book there somewhere'

Gail and Christopher Lawther – who else could make all this work seem like fun while coordinating it so professionally?

Juliet Webster, who invited me, along with many other British quilters, to put our heads above the parapet

Dianne Huck and Christine Porter – encouragement is their key word

Dorothy Stapleton and Angela Besley, for telling me to 'go for it' when this book was but a twinkle

Lesley Porter and Puddleducks quilt shop for their support, and loan of fabrics for photography

All of my students and visitors to quilt shows, for their interest, and for continually asking me 'Where's the book?' Well, here it is!

Additional thanks to Traplet Publications and Teamwork Craftbooks for putting their faith in me; Hilary Williams of The Silk Route, Stef Francis (Threads) and Craft Creations Ltd for their generous sponsorships

Suppliers in the UK

- Stef Francis (mail order)
Waverley, High Rocombe,
Stokeinteignhead, Newton Abbot,
Devon TQ12 4QL
Tel 01803 323004
e-mail: sales@stef-francis.co.uk
website: www.stef-francis.co.uk
space-dyed fabrics and threads

- The Silk Route (mail order)
Cross Cottage, Cross Lane,
Frimley Green, Surrey GU16 6LN
Tel 01252 835781
e-mail: hilary@thesilkroute.co.uk
website: www.thesilkroute.co.uk
textured silk, threads

- Craft Creations Ltd (mail order)
Ingersoll House, Delamare Road,
Cheshunt, Herts TQ12 4QL
Tel 01992 781900
e-mail: enquiries@craftcreations.com
website: www.craftcreations.com
aperture cards, envelopes

- Out of Africa (mail order)
17 Bashford Way,
Crawley, Sussex RH10 7YF
e-mail: outofafrica@tinyonline.co.uk
dyed and painted fabrics

- Glitterati
Unit 1, Staples Corner Business Park,
Suite 9, Big Yellow Offices,
1000 North Circular Road,
London NW2 7JP
Tel 020 7723 5556
mixed shisha (mirrors) and beads

- Fingerwrap thimbles
- *Texture by Design*
(A4 black-and-white booklet)
- *Quilting With A Difference*
(follow-up video)
All available from:
Nikki Tinkler,
22 Aperfield Road,
Biggin Hill, Kent TN16 3LU
Tel 01959 574604
e-mail: nikki@jtinkler.freeserve.co.uk
website: www.nikkitinkler.com

Specialist patchwork and quilting supplies

- Puddleducks
116 St John's Hill,
Sevenoaks, Kent TN13 3PD
Tel 01732 743642
supplies include fabrics, notions, books etc

- The Quilt Room
20 West Street
Dorking
Surrey RH4 1BL
Tel 01306 877307
e-mail: sales@quiltroom.co.uk
website: www.quiltroom.co.uk
supplies include soft leather thimbles, and stencils

- The Cotton Patch
1285 Stratford Road,
Hall Green, Birmingham B28 9AJ
Tel 0121 702 2840
e-mail: mailorder@cottonpatch.net
website: www.cottonpatch.net
supplies include wire S hooks and quilt hangers